••• **Trainer's Manual**

The
CELTA
Certificate in English Language Teaching to Adults
Course

Scott Thornbury

Peter Watkins

Published in collaboration with Cambridge ESOL

UNIVERSITY *of* CAMBRIDGE
ESOL Examinations

English for Speakers of Other Languages

CAMBRIDGE
UNIVERSITY PRESS

CAMBRIDGE UNIVERSITY PRESS
Cambridge, New York, Melbourne, Madrid, Cape Town, Singapore, São Paulo, Delhi

Cambridge University Press
The Edinburgh Building, Cambridge CB2 8RU, UK

www.cambridge.org
Information on this title: www.cambridge.org/9780521692076

First published 2007
Reprinted 2007

Printed in the United Kingdom by Polestar Wheatons

A catalogue record for this publication is available from the British Library

ISBN 978-0-521-69207-6 paperback

Contents

Introduction

What is *The CELTA Course?*

The CELTA Course is a coursebook for participants on the CELTA course. (For more on CELTA, visit the Cambridge ESOL website: http://www.cambridgeesol.org/.) The course covers all the main content areas addressed in CELTA and aims to provide trainers with ready-made session plans that can be tailored to meet the needs of their trainees. It thus saves on preparation time, as well as reducing the need to prepare and copy session handouts. It also provides a basis around which new centres can design and structure their courses. Finally, it provides trainees with a compact record of their course, which they can consult both during the course and afterwards.

What does *The CELTA Course* consist of?

The CELTA Course consists of two components:

- *Trainee Book*: this includes material to be used in input sessions on the course, plus advice concerning the practical and administrative aspects of the course, along with a file of useful reference material.
- *Trainer's Manual*: this includes guidance and advice as to how best to exploit the material in the Trainee Book, as well as photocopiable material to supplement sessions.

The bulk of the course comprises forty units, each representing an input session of between 45 to 90 minutes. The selection of topic areas for these units reflects the choice of topics in the sample CELTA timetable (available on the Cambridge ESOL website). This timetable is in turn a synthesis of a number of timetables that were submitted by different CELTA centres worldwide.

The 40 units are divided into four topic areas:

- Section A: The learners and their contexts
  (Units 1 and 2) Learners' purposes, goals, expectations and learning styles
- Section B: Classroom teaching
  (Units 3–26) Presenting language, developing language skills, planning, classroom management, teaching different levels, English for special purposes, monitoring and assessing learning, choosing and using teaching resources
- Section C: Language analysis and awareness
  (Units 27–39) Grammar, vocabulary and pronunciation
- Section D: Professional development
  (Unit 40) How to get a job and continue your professional development

The division of topics into these four areas means that the sequence of topic areas in the book does *not* exactly match the sequence in the sample CELTA timetable. The sequencing of topics in the book has been governed by a number of factors. These include:

- *Developmental*: topics considered to be more fundamental – such as classroom management – are dealt with before topics that can be safely postponed until later in the course – such as teaching ESP or exam classes.
- *Thematic*: topic areas that are related are usually sequenced together.

- *Convention:* topics that – for whatever reasons – are conventionally dealt with early in most courses precede those that are conventionally dealt with later.

However, it is not expected that trainers will follow the sequence of topics in exactly the order that they are presented. (For more on how to use the course, see below.)

Each unit comprises a number of tasks, starting with a warm-up task and concluding with a reflection task. For some units, optional tasks are available in the Trainer's Manual, with photocopiable materials, where necessary.

As well as the input session tasks, the Trainee Book includes the following features:

- Teaching practice: This section consists of practical advice for trainees as well as a bank of TP reflection tasks.
- Classroom observation: This section consists of a bank of observation tasks for use in observing experienced teachers (as part of the course requirements) and also teaching practice (TP).
- Written assignments and tutorials: This section includes advice as to how trainees should interpret the assessment criteria and how they can best prepare for tutorials.
- Resource file: This section includes:
  - an overview of the main verb forms
  - a bank of warmers and games
  - a glossary
  - recommended reading list and relevant website addresses

The Trainer's Manual consists of:

- a guide for each unit, on how to set up activities, suggested variants and expected answers to tasks
- optional (photocopiable) materials for some units
- teaching practice: some guidelines on how to organise TP, write TP points and give TP feedback
- classroom observation: some suggestions as to how to get the most out of this component of the course
- introductory photocopiable quiz
- a photocopiable review boardgame for trainees

How should *The CELTA Course* be used?

Each CELTA centre will design and run its courses according to its own particular circumstances and needs. Hence, *The CELTA Course* has been designed with flexibility and adaptability in mind. Course trainers are invited to select only those elements that meet the needs and syllabus specifications of their particular courses: it is not expected, for example, that they will do *all* the units and *all* the tasks in the book (for one thing, there is unlikely to be sufficient time on most courses), nor that they will do the units in the order that they occur in the book. To this end, the units have been written as far as possible as stand alone entities.

When using the material, however, trainers should observe certain core principles that are intrinsic to the CELTA scheme. These are that the course is:

- **Practical**: The CELTA is an introductory course and as such it has to be very practical. This does not mean avoiding theoretical issues, but simply that input sessions should always be firmly grounded in classroom practice. This may mean starting with a discussion of classroom experiences, drawing out some basic principles and returning to classroom practice through the analysis and evaluation of classroom materials.

- **Integrated**: In keeping with the above point, emphasising the interconnectedness, not only of theory and practice, but also of the different strands of the course, should be a priority. These strands include the input sessions, TP, classroom observation and the written assignments. Trainers should seek every opportunity to draw connections and to encourage trainees to make these connections for themselves. One way of doing this, for example, is to adapt some tasks so that they anticipate forthcoming teaching practice points, or to choose, as example material, extracts from the coursebooks the trainees are using in their TP. Likewise, TP reflection tasks and classroom observation tasks can be chosen so that they tie in with areas of content that have been dealt with – or are about to be dealt with – in the input sessions. Likewise, opportunities to recycle themes that have been dealt with at an earlier stage in the course should be exploited. For example, when dealing with an area of language awareness, such as tense and aspect, there will be opportunities to review approaches to grammar presentation and practice.
- **Experiential**: Axiomatic to the CELTA course is the notion that learning is optimised if it is driven by personal experience. To this end, trainers are recommended to include demonstrations of classroom procedures in the sessions, where the trainees experience classroom techniques as learners, and reflect on their experience. Many of the tasks in the book can be substituted with actual demonstrations and these opportunities are flagged in the Trainer's Manual.
- **Co-operative**: The course has been prepared for classroom use (as opposed to self-study) and as such exploits the communal and collaborative nature of the CELTA, where trainees frequently work together in pairs or small groups in order to compare experiences, solve tasks, debate issues, evaluate materials, or design lessons. For each task, the Trainer's Manual suggests an appropriate organisation. Typically, this organisation will take the form of pairwork or small-group work, followed by some kind of report-back stage. It is important that the training should take place in a space that is conducive to a variety of different formations and interactions.
- **Reflective**: A key component of the experiential learning cycle is reflection: for this reason every unit ends with a reflection task. But reflection can be built into the course at other points too. For example, after trainees have experienced an activity as if they were learners, they can then reflect on their experience in order to extrapolate principles that might apply when setting up the same or similar activities as teachers.

A good idea, on Day 1, is to give the trainees a light-hearted quiz about the course, its administration, and about your institution. They can answer this individually and then compare in pairs or groups. Alternatively, it could be done as a race with groups competing with each other to finish it first. They should be allowed to consult their books and any other related handouts in search of the answers.

A suggested quiz can be found in this book on page 179. Trainers may of course want to design their own quiz material.

1 Who are the learners?

> **Main focus**
> To raise awareness regarding the learners, their backgrounds, their level of comprehension and production.
>
> **Learning outcomes**
> - Trainees are aware of the diversity of learner purposes, goals, expectations, and degree of motivation.
> - Trainees can describe different levels of proficiency in general terms.
> - Trainees understand the importance of identifying and accommodating learner differences.
>
> **Key concepts**
> - purposes, goals, expectations, motivation
> - English as a foreign language (EFL), English as a second language (ESL), English as an international language (EIL), English for specific purposes (ESP)
> - acquisition vs learning
> - monolingualism, bilingualism and multilingualism

Stage	Focus
A Warm-up	reflecting on a previous second language learning experience
B Learners' purposes	identifying the different purposes for learning English
C Learners' goals	distinguishing between different goals
D Learners' expectations	relating learners' expectations to their background
Reflection	thinking of questions to ask to (or about) the learners

Note: It is expected that this session will take place prior to the trainees meeting their teaching practice classes for the first time. If this is not possible, it should be scheduled as near to the start of the teaching practice as possible, so that trainees can get the maximum benefit from the diagnostic task (see **Reflection**).

A Warm-up

You could begin this stage by briefly relating a language learning experience of your own. Organise the class into groups to share their experiences. The objective of the activity is to identify context factors that impact on learning, particularly the learners' purposes, achievement goals, expectations and degree of motivation. At the end of the discussion, elicit examples of widely differing learning experiences.

An alternative way of introducing this activity is to set up a 'Find someone who....' activity, with trainees milling in order to ask and answer questions to find trainees who share certain language learning experiences. Photocopy and distribute the following rubric:

Find someone who:

- speaks at least two other languages fluently
- is bilingual
- taught themselves a second language
- picked up a second language simply by living in the country where it is spoken
- studied a second language at school but didn't enjoy the experience

B Learners' purposes

Ask trainees to read the profiles and identify the learners' reasons for learning English. These are, in general terms:

- Ning Wang – to pass an exam, and then to study in English
- Lucia – probably no immediate purpose
- Kazankiran and Maxim – integration into an English-speaking society, including work and education
- Soni Kim – travel
- Carmen – business
- Mies – academic study.

1 You could write up the abbreviations (EFL, ESL, etc.) on the board, and ask trainees if they know what they stand for. Trainees then identify the one that best matches each situation. (You may like to do the first one with them.) Answers: Ning Wang: EFL, EAP; Lucia: EFL; Kazankiran: ESL; Maxim: ESL; Soni Kim: EFL; Carmen: ESP, EIL; Mies: EAP, EIL. Note that the term ESOL (= English for speakers of other languages) is widely used to cover both EFL and ESL.

Note that none of these terms is unproblematic, and that the point of the matching activity is to problematise them, to a certain extent. The difference between *foreign* and *second* is not always obvious; and for many learners English is not their *second* but perhaps their *third* or *fourth* language (which is why the acronym EAL – *English as an additional language* – is sometimes preferred). Also, now that English has global language status, it is likely that the EFL/EIL distinction will become blurred, to the point of being irrelevant. (ESP is dealt with in more detail in *Classroom Teaching* Session 22.)

The next three questions introduce key concepts in language acquisition:

2 The nearest to a pure bilingual (i.e. someone who has two 'first' languages) is perhaps Mies, (Dutch and English), but it could also be argued that all these learners are bilingual (or multilingual) in that they have (some degree of) competence in more than one language. Since Kazankiran already speaks two languages, the addition of English will make her multilingual. It is worth pointing out that bilingualism/multilingualism is a more 'normal' condition than monolingualism: for many learners, English will not be even a second language.

3 All things being equal, the closer the first language and the second language are – in terms of vocabulary, grammar, script, and pronunciation – the more likely the former will aid the learning of the latter. Thus, Lucia's Italian, Carmen's Portuguese and Mies's Dutch will contribute more to their English learning than, say, Soni Kim's Korean, or Kazankiran's Kurdish and Arabic.

4 The distinction between (intentional) *learning*, e.g. in a classroom context, and (incidental) *acquisition* is a useful one, but, again, easily blurred. The clearest instance of acquisition in these profiles is Maxim. Both Ning Wang and Kazankiran are attending classes, but they are probably also picking up English by virtue of living in an English-speaking context. This is not the case with Carmen or Soni Kim, who are closer to the learning end of the spectrum. Mies started English at such an early age that he probably picked up (i.e. acquired) more language than he learnt formally, at least initially.

5 Those living in an English-speaking environment (Kazankiran, Ning Wang, and Maxim) will be getting the most exposure, but this may be limited, depending on the contact they have with English-speakers. Mies will also be getting a lot of exposure, although more to non-native speakers than native speakers perhaps. Soni Kim is probably getting the least exposure, since Carmen probably already uses her English in her business dealings, and Lucia is attending classes both at school and after school. All of the case studies (except perhaps for Soni Kim) are *users* to some extent. Even Lucia could be said to be putting her language knowledge to use, even if this is in a classroom context. This suggests that labelling learners as, simply, *learners*, masks the fact that many of them are already using English, maybe in ways that do not always reflect the content and pace of their formal learning.

6 Without more information, it is hard to say who is likely to be motivated or not. Motivation is a rather personal attribute, and is not necessarily a result of having a clear purpose (or motive) for learning, although this certainly helps. The extent that the learning experience fulfils the learners' expectations will also contribute to their motivation.

7 The answer to this question will obviously depend on the particular circumstances of the trainees, but it is likely that most of them will be anticipating teaching in (adult) EFL, rather than ESL, contexts, and to groups rather than one-to-one or online.

C Learners' goals

The point of this section is to introduce criteria for establishing learning goals, and to suggest that different learners will have different goals, in terms of the level of proficiency they wish (or need) to achieve. The concept of *partial competence* may be sufficient for many.

1 a Maxim; b Kazankiran; c Soni Kim; d Carmen.
2 Soni Kim and Maxim are at the basic user end of the scale, while Carmen probably aims to be an independent user and Kazankiran a proficient user. Note that these terms are borrowed from the *Common European Framework of Reference for Languages* (CEF), a 'detailed model for describing and scaling language use'.

D Learners' expectations

1 Ning Wang expected a more traditional, teacher-controlled, accuracy-focused classroom.
2 The type of classroom he was used to in China.
3 Given the exam-orientation of the course he is attending, these expectations could be considered realistic.
4 Despite Lucia's expectations (based on her school experience) not being met, she was happy since the less formal, learner-centred approach of her evening classes probably seemed appropriate.
5 The notion of *appropriacy* is probably more important than simply trying to match instruction to learners' expectations. The new approach was more appropriate for Lucia than for Ning Wang.

REFLECTION

1 Ideally, this task should be prepared in advance of the trainees meeting their teaching practice classes for the first time. The trainees can then conduct interviews with their teaching practice students: if there are more students than trainees in these classes, the interviews can take place in small groups. The number of questions will depend on the level of the classes, but, in any case, they should be quite broad, offering learners plenty of opportunity to speak. E.g. 'Tell me about your English classes at school in ….'

2 If it is not possible for trainees to interview the students, the questions can be directed at you, as long as you know who will be in the teaching practice classes.

2 Learners as individuals

Main focus

To raise awareness about the individual needs of learners and how these needs can be accommodated.

Learning outcomes

- Trainees are aware of the diversity of learner purposes, goals, expectations and degree of motivation.
- Trainees can describe different levels of proficiency in general terms.
- Trainees understand the importance of identifying and accommodating learner differences.

Key concepts

- learning styles, multiple intelligences
- learning strategies, learner training
- learner autonomy, individualised instruction

Stage	Focus
A Warm-up	reflecting on learner differences
B Learning style	identifying different learning styles
C Multiple intelligences	identifying different kinds of intelligence
D Learning strategies and learner training	identifying learning strategies and evaluating learner training approaches
E Learner autonomy	exploring ways of developing learner autonomy
Reflection	summarising ways of dealing with diversity

Note that this session should be timetabled only when the trainees are already familiar with their teaching practice students.

A Warm-up

Trainees can perform this reflective task in pairs or small groups. Ideally, they should work with other members of their teaching practice group, so that they share a familiarity with the learners. Note that some of the differences they identify may relate to the context factors discussed in Unit A1, such as previous learning experience and motivation. A brief review of this session may be helpful.

B Learning style

1 Characteristics of a passive–experiential learning style (type C) might be: they enjoy the social aspects of learning, and like to learn from experience, but more as observers than active participants; type D learners, on the other hand, are willing to take risks, are not afraid of making mistakes, and prefer direct communication rather than analysis and study of rules.

2 Trainees can work on this task in pairs or small groups. Some typical questions might be:
- How do you feel when your teacher corrects you?
- Do you like games and groupwork in class?
- Do you try to speak English outside the classroom?
- How often do you read in English?
- How often do you watch English movies?
- Do you note down new words when you read them?
- Do you review your English lessons?
- Do you always do your homework?

Note: If trainees have the opportunity, they could use their questionnaires in their teaching practice classes, and use the data to feed into their 'Focus on the learner' assignment.

C Multiple intelligences

Note: As well as the intelligences listed, other intelligences, such as *emotional intelligence*, *natural intelligence* and *spiritual intelligence* have been proposed. You could also point out that classroom activities involving movement and physical contact may not go down well in certain contexts.

1 The activity is designed to foster interpersonal intelligence. There is also a kinesthetic element, perhaps, since it involves touch and movement.
2 You can make this task easier by suggesting that trainees consult their coursebooks to find activities that might match the different intelligences.
- *visual intelligence*: anything involving images, e.g. visual aids, video, learners drawing (e.g. a picture that is dictated to them)
- *kinesthetic intelligence*: activities involving movement, e.g. action games (like *Simon says…*), 'Total Physical Response' techniques, drama activities, etc.
- *musical intelligence*: listening to and singing songs; jazz chants; background music (as in Suggestopedia).

D Learning strategies and learner training

1 1 The areas of language learning that these strategies focus on are:
   Learner A: pronunciation, particularly intonation; memorising chunks of language
   Learner B: vocabulary
   Learner C: speaking/interacting
   Learner D: reading
2 The learning principles involved might be:
   A: repetition aids memory, at least in the short term; subvocalisation helps pronunciation
   B: forming associations aids memory
   C: interaction is necessary for language learning; collaboration aids learning
   D: using 'top-down' processes such as guessing meaning from context improves reading fluency
2 The extracts target:
   A: vocabulary learning
   B: dictionary use, for both pronunciation and meaning
   C: note-taking and record-keeping, especially of vocabulary

3 You may prefer to assign one extract per group, and then have groups report back. Possible ways of exploiting these extracts include:

A: demonstrating the use of word cards in class; asking learners to prepare their own and to show them to each other; testing each other; including a word-card writing and testing slot in each lesson, at least initially, until learners are in the habit.

B: distributing dictionaries and asking learners to work together to find the meanings and pronunciation of unfamiliar words; asking them to group words that rhyme, using the dictionary; using dictionaries to choose between similar words to fit a context, e.g. commuter, computer.

C: completing a verb chart; dictating verbs that learners then record in their notebooks, along with their pronunciation; asking learners to 'proof-read' each other's vocabulary records; reviewing their notes in later lessons and asking them to pronounce the words to each other.

E Learner autonomy

Before this activity, elicit the different kinds of reference sources that are targeted at learners, such as grammar reference books, dictionaries (print, on-line, CD; monolingual, bilingual, picture, specialised, etc.), vocabulary exercise books, the reference sections of their coursebooks, CD-ROMs and internet grammar sites. Then, elicit as many different ways in which learners might have exposure to English, even in non-English speaking contexts, e.g. films, TV, songs, books, newspapers and magazines, adverts, internet (including sound files, video, etc.), computer games, tourists, etc. Trainees can use these lists to help brainstorm ideas in order to make suggestions for each of the questions. Some possible ideas:

a Read graded readers; magazines targeted at learners; literature written for English-speaking children or teenagers; short authentic texts about topics they are familiar with.

b Listen to songs where the lyrics are available, watch videos with English subtitles; download short news reports from the internet, and read their associated news story.

c Watch movies with English subtitles, rather than L1 subtitles; record movies and watch short segments repeatedly, perhaps with a copy of the script, if available; choose movies that are based on a novel or a play, and read the book in advance, especially if it's available in a simplified form (e.g. classics such as *Pride and Prejudice*); avoid films whose English is very vernacular, regional, etc.

d Probably not; alternatives are learning words that come up in reading texts, or at least learning from lists of high frequency words (such as the *defining words* found at the back of most learner's dictionaries).

e Find grammar sites on the internet, buy a grammar reference book with exercises (e.g. *English Grammar in Use* by Raymond Murphy, CUP); use the exercises in the coursebook and the workbook.

f Start a blog; find sites dedicated to learners; join a chat room; use the reference material available, including corpus sites; download the lyrics of songs, extracts of films, reading and listening material, etc. (For further ideas, see *The Internet and the Language Classroom* by Gavin Dudeney, CUP.)

g Use pronunciation materials; join an English-speaking club; have a conversation exchange with an English speaker who wants to learn your language; record yourself speaking, etc.

REFLECTION

Organise trainees into groups and distribute materials to make posters or projections. Points that might come up are:

DO	DON'T
diagnose learners' needs, interests, learning styles, goals, etc.	treat learners as if they were all the same
provide a range of different activity types, topics etc.	use the same approach all the time, e.g. to teaching grammar or practising vocabulary
offer choices, and involve the learners in making decisions about the materials, activities, etc.	use the coursebook all the time
help learners make the best use of their learning style/intelligence	expect all learners to work comfortably at the same pace and rhythm
show learners how to take advantage of opportunities for learning outside the classroom	ignore learner resistance or frustrations
teach specific strategies to improve learning (learner training)	assume everyone learns in the same way that you do
mix and match learners, providing different opportunities for collaboration and interaction	
provide individual assistance and counselling where possible	
get feedback on the learning process at regular intervals	

3 Foreign language lesson

<table>
<tr><td>Main focus
Trainees have a lesson in a foreign language.

Learning outcomes<ul><li>Trainees experience learning a language.</li><li>Trainees reflect on their learning experience.</li></ul></td><td>Key concepts<ul><li>classroom management, instructions, seating</li><li>involvement, participation, interaction</li><li>staging, aims</li><li>clarifying meaning, comprehension</li><li>language similarities and differences</li></ul></td></tr>
</table>

Stage	Focus
A Warm-up	sharing experiences to predict what may happen in the lesson
B A foreign language lesson	experiencing a lesson in a foreign language
C After your lesson	considering what happened in the lesson and how it affected feelings
D Comparing languages	comparing the new language and English
Reflection	reflecting on what has been experienced

Note: You may wish to have a separate teacher for the foreign language lesson itself, Section B.

A Warm-up

The aim of this section is to get learners to think about what may happen in the lesson and to anticipate some of the techniques and procedures that may be used. The trainees could talk to each other in small groups about their experiences before reporting back in open class.

B A foreign language lesson

This is obviously the most important part of the session. There is no 'right' lesson to teach, or 'right' way of approaching it. It is important that whoever teaches the lesson feels comfortable with what they are doing. The lesson does not necessarily have to be taught by one of the trainers on the course. Here are some general points to consider in preparing the lesson:

- The lesson should probably last around 30 minutes.
- The lesson should be predominantly in the target language.
- Learners should be given the opportunity to speak and to interact, as far as possible.
- The teacher may want to correct some errors in order to provide a model of error correction for trainees.
- The teacher should maintain a natural speaking voice and speed of delivery, even if using simplified language.

Here are two lesson plans that you could use as a model for your language lesson, if you wish:

Note: In these lesson plans, the language forms are given in English, but their target language equivalents should obviously be used throughout.

Lesson 1

Aim: *What's your name? My name is …*
- Teacher writes his/her name on the board.
- Teacher models *My name is X.*
- Teacher asks a trainee *What's your name?*

(The trainee is unlikely to understand this – but may guess from the context what you want them to say – be prepared to help by modelling the language again.)

- Continue to nominate other trainees – each time they should use *My name is …*
- Be prepared to correct pronunciation that is very inaccurate and would interfere with understanding.

By now the trainees will have heard *What's your name?* several times.

- Model it again and ask for choral repetition.
- Ask for some individual repetition.
- Write both *What's your name?* and *My name is …* on the board.
- Gesture that trainees should copy this down.
- Ask one of the trainees to repeat the question after you – and answer it yourself.
- Ask the same trainee to ask the question – this time directing it to another class member.
- Continue this – with the person answering the question, being the next person to ask the question.
- Ask the trainees to stand up. Ask them to mingle around the room asking and answering the question as many times as they can.
- Stop the activity. Ask one or two trainees the question, *What's your name?* to finish the lesson.

If you wish to extend the lesson you could:

- Collect pictures of famous people from different countries. For each person you need the flag which represents their country.
- Use the flags to teach the vocabulary of the countries. You could use both individual and choral repetition. Write the new words on the board.
- Drill the question *Where are you from?*
- Give out the pictures and the corresponding flag.
- Ask a trainee their new 'name'. Ask them where they are from. For example:
  Teacher: What's your name?
  Trainee: Kylie
  Teacher: Where are you from?
  Trainee: Australia
- Set up some pairwork to practise this routine.

Lesson 2

Aim: *I like … I don't like …*

- Use realia and/or pictures to teach four or five items of vocabulary, such as chocolate, apples, lemonade, tomatoes and cheese.
- Hold up the first object/picture. Model the word.

- Ask everyone to repeat it together.
- Ask for some individual repetition.
- Continue with the other objects/pictures.
- Hold up the first picture again. Re-elicit the word and write it on the board.
- Do the same for the other items.
- Gesture that the trainees should write the words down.
- Use a gesture, or draw a smiling face on the board and add *I like* before one of the items – *I like apples*.
- Use choral and individual repetition.
- Use a gesture, or draw a frowning face on the board and add *I don't like* before one of the items – *I don't like lemonade*.
- Use choral and individual repetition.
- Use some fairly universal brand names such as Coca-Cola, McDonald's, Guinness (assuming that alcohol is not inappropriate for the culture you are in) and Pizza Hut to expand your vocabulary list without adding to the learning load.
- Draw the following on the board – putting your name and the name of one of the trainees.

		Jane	
		likes	doesn't like
Don	likes		Guinness
	doesn't like		

The aim is to find something you both like, something neither of you likes and something that each of you like that the other doesn't. For example:

Teacher (Don): I like Guinness. Do you?
Trainee (Jane): Sorry?
Teacher: Guinness?
Trainee: No
Teacher indicates the phrase – I don't like
Trainee: I don't like Guinness.
Teacher: OK [writes 'Guinness' on the grid]

- Divide the trainees into pairs. They should copy the grid and complete it by saying what they like and don't like.
- Ask individual trainees to report back.

If you wish to extend the lesson you could[1]:

- Teach the phrases: *I like it, I don't like it* and *it's OK*. You could use both individual and choral repetition. Write the new words on the board.
- Prepare a recording of short extracts of very varied music.
- Play each piece of music and ask the trainees to comment on each one, using the phrases above.

---

[1] This activity is based on one in the *New Cambridge English Course 1*, Michael Swan and Catherine Walter, Cambridge University Press.

C After your lesson

It may be useful to have a different person conduct feedback than the person who taught the lesson. This may allow trainees to speak more freely, less worried that they may make an implicit criticism of their teacher.

The trainees are likely to be quite energised after their learning experience and the concentration it requires. You may like to have a short break (say five minutes or so), or at least allow the trainees to discuss their feelings in a fairly unstructured way for a short time before focusing them on some of the questions given, if necessary.

You may wish to follow up the questions in the trainee book with some more specific questions, such as:

- **setting up activities**
  How did the teacher explain instructions?
  How did the teacher end activities?
- **involving the learners**
  Did you repeat things that your teacher said? If so, did you feel this was useful?
  Did you have to speak in front of the rest of the class? How did you feel?
- **making meaning clear**
  Was there anything you didn't understand in the lesson?
  Were you able to ask for clarification?
- **presenting new words or expressions**
  Did your teacher write anything on the board? If so, what?
  Would you have liked more time to write things down?
- **dealing with errors**
  Did the teacher correct any errors? If so, what and how? Was the amount of correction about right during the lesson? Would you have liked more/less?

You might also like to encourage trainees to discuss the extent to which they actually used, or would have liked to use, English. They could also discuss whether the teacher used any English and if so, in what situations and for what purposes.

D Comparing languages

Allow trainees to discuss this briefly in pairs before asking them to report back in open class. You may need to point things out for them, and could mention the implications this would have for learning/teaching. For example, the length of time it may take learners to become confident with certain features of the language. However, it is worth pointing out that by no means all difficulties or errors are caused by divergence between languages.

REFLECTION

Trainees could discuss these questions in small groups before you ask them to report back in open class. How much they remember may depend on their motivation to remember (unlikely to be great, as they have no real reason to learn the language). In order to remember, they would need to review what they have learned at home, look for opportunities to practise, and so on. You may like to focus the discussion of questions 2 and 3 by considering what specific things they could do (or not do) in teaching practice during the course.

4 Classroom management

Main focus

To examine some of the principal considerations in classroom management and in facilitating interaction.

Learning outcomes

- Trainees understand the rationale behind the use of different seating arrangements.
- Trainees understand the rationale behind the use of pairwork and groupwork.
- Trainees understand how to use the board.
- Trainees understand the principles of how to grade language and give instructions.
- Trainees understand the principles of effective monitoring.

Key concepts

- classroom organisation, seating, monitoring
- boardwork
- language grading, teacher talk
- instructions

Stage	Focus
A Warm-up	introducing some background issues in classroom management
B Classroom organisation	considering different seating arrangements, and the use of the board
C Grading language	looking at ways of making classroom language intelligible
D Giving instructions	introducing the main considerations in giving clear instructions
E Trainees' questions	trainees match questions and answers on a variety of practical points
F Classroom application	trainees consider the implications of what they have learned for their own teaching
Reflection	trainees review some of the main terms used in talking about classroom management

Note: This unit can serve only as an introduction to classroom management, and you will probably want to return to the issues as trainees gain more teaching experience.

A Warm-up

a Gesture

Gestures are used to support communication and the classroom is no different in this respect. Typically teachers need to use a lot of gesture, and developing a repertoire of easily understood gestures (such as pointing over your shoulder to indicate the past) can help to cut down on the amount of verbal explanation teachers are required to give and consequently the processing burden placed on learners, particularly at lower levels.

b Pointing

Suggest that, as an alternative to pointing, it is a good idea to learn learners' names. You may also like to show trainees less aggressive gestures that could be used instead of pointing.

c Silence

If people are to practise speaking they need to speak, for example during pairwork and groupwork, and this will create some noise. However, teachers need to distinguish between 'useful' noise and 'disruptive' noise.

d Hands up

More appropriate to young learners than to adults.

e Demonstration

Especially at lower levels, explanation is likely to challenge learners' ability to understand; also, some classroom activities may be unfamiliar to them, and are best demonstrated.

B Classroom organisation

1 It might be worth pointing out to trainees that seating arrangements are sometimes beyond the control of the teacher. Where the teacher can control the arrangements:

- *a large class*: for very large classes, arrangement (1) may be the only alternative, although, depending on the size of the room, other arrangements – such as (2) and (4) – may be viable.
- *a small, business English class*: arrangement (3) is ideal, not least because it reflects the 'meeting' format that these learners may be used to.
- *a grammar presentation*: arrangements (1) and (2) may be best because this usually requires attention on the teacher and the board; arrangement (3) would also work for small groups.
- *pairwork*: all formats can easily be adapted for pairwork.
- *groupwork*. arrangement (4) is obviously ideal, but with a little re-organisation the other formats can be adapted for groupwork too. For example, in (1) pairs in one row can turn to face pairs in the row behind them.
- *an exam*: probably (1), especially if the learners are separated.

2 1 Answers will vary. It's likely that some activities were done in pairs or groups, but the purpose of each pair and group stage will depend on the lesson given.

2 Pairwork and groupwork maximise the opportunities learners have to use the language productively, giving lots of speaking opportunities. They also allow learners to practise without having to perform in front of the whole class, and this may help them to build confidence. In addition, pairwork and groupwork allow learners to use a relatively informal style, whereas some may feel the need to be relatively more formal if addressing the teacher.

3 In some classes, particularly large ones, pair- and groupwork can lead to a loss of teacher control and a sense of disorder. Learners may be uneasy if they feel that the teacher cannot hear what they are saying and that a lot of errors are going uncorrected. Indeed, the idea of pair- and groupwork may run contrary to the expectations of some learners. Unobserved by the teacher, learners may resort to the easiest means of achieving the task, including the use of their first language. However, most teachers tend to feel that the benefits outweigh these potential drawbacks.

3 Use the pictures to help the trainees understand the most effective way of using the board. The following points could be made:
- Plan the use of the board, perhaps leaving designated spaces for different purposes.
- Use upper and lower case appropriately.
- Take care with spelling.
- Generally avoid joined up writing as it is harder to read.
- Generally avoid letting the board become too cluttered.

If you prefer, you could create a poor example on the board yourself and ask trainees how it could be improved.

C Grading language

It is important to point out that it is not necessary for learners to understand every individual word that the teacher says. But it is important that the learners understand enough to comprehend the overall message. Most researchers agree that such 'comprehensible input' is a necessary (if not sufficient) condition for language acquisition to take place.

The advice centres on making language easier to understand because most trainees have more difficulty in grading language appropriately for lower-level learners than higher-level learners, where they can speak making fewer adjustments to their language.

Good advice	Potentially unsound advice
b Use gestures, pictures and other things that will support what you are saying to make it easier to understand. c Speak with natural rhythm and intonation. e Speak at a natural speed, but pause slightly longer after each 'chunk', if necessary. *A little extra decoding time after each phrase is likely to help comprehension more than pausing after each word.* f Try to avoid 'difficult' vocabulary (for example, very idiomatic language). g Try to avoid complex grammar patterns.	a Pronounce each word slowly and deliberately. *Learners need to get used to hearing reasonably natural sounding language.* d Miss out small words (articles, prepositions, auxiliary verbs and so on) so that learners can focus on the 'content' words and understand the message. *This will impoverish the input they receive – learners pick up a lot of grammar from hearing it used.* *Also, learners may feel patronised if they feel they are being spoken to in 'babytalk'.*

D Giving instructions

1 Rather than having the trainees read descriptions given here, you may prefer to demonstrate by giving two sets of instructions to the trainees for an activity. This may be more involving for the trainees.

The second set of instructions is easier to understand. This should be very easy to spot. Trainees may comment on:

Teacher 2 breaks down the instructions – only telling learners what they need to know for the next part of the lesson and therefore placing less burden on memory.

Teacher 2 is more direct – Compare: 'if you wouldn't mind …' with 'Write four sentences, please'. (Imperative forms + 'please' are useful for many instructions.)

Teacher 1 is less explicit – 'or threes if you want' and doesn't tell learners who they should work with.

Teacher 2 uses the material to make instructions clearer (pointing to the pictures, in this case).

Teacher 1 uses quite demanding vocabulary, e.g. *have a go, have in common, mingle.*

Teacher 2 checks understanding more effectively, e.g. *do you speak to one person or lots?*

2 The bullet points are intended to give a summary of these points. You might also like to point out that it can sometimes be useful for teachers to check that learners have understood the instructions for a task by asking simple questions.

E Trainees' queries

1 Ask trainees to read the comments and to discuss possible solutions to the problems.
2 Ask them to do the matching activity, to compare their answers, and to compare them with their own solutions in 1, above. Suggested answers: 1–d) 2–f) 3–b) 4–a) 5–c) 6–e).
3 Be ready to answer any other questions that the trainees may have.

F Classroom application

You need to ensure that trainees know what lesson they will next be teaching before you do this section.

Allow the trainees to think about the prompts given. Or, if you are short of time, ask them to choose the point that they feel is most relevant to them. You could then put the trainees into small groups to share ideas and suggestions before asking them to report back briefly in open class.

REFLECTION

Give an example of good advice based on the terms. For example, 'Decide on the seating arrangement that is most appropriate to the size of the class and to the kind of activity you have planned.' Allow the trainees time to complete the task, working in pairs or small groups. Check their understanding of some of the terms, and elicit examples of good advice.

5 Presenting vocabulary

Main focus
Ways of presenting vocabulary.

Learning outcomes
- Trainees understand some ways of conveying the meaning of new lexical items.
- Trainees understand the basic principles of eliciting new language from learners.
- Trainees understand the basic principles of checking the understanding of new language.

Key concepts
- word knowledge: meaning, spoken and written form, use
- conveying meaning: visual aids, realia, mime, demonstration, definition
- eliciting
- checking understanding; concept checking

Stage	Focus
A Warm-up	introducing the topic
B Form, meaning and use	introducing the need to learn form and meaning
C Learning about form and meaning	introducing some vocabulary teaching techniques
D Eliciting vocabulary	introducing basic principles for eliciting new language
E Checking understanding	introducing concept checking questions
F Practising vocabulary	trainees are introduced to three ways of practising vocabulary
G Classroom application: microteaching	trainees have the opportunity to experiment with the techniques introduced
Reflection	trainees reflect on what they have learned

There is one optional activty for this unit, about analysing a vocabulary activity.

There is a lot of material in this unit. If your timetable allows, you may prefer to split it into more than one session. Alternatively, concept-checking could be omitted here and covered during Unit 7, where it also occurs. It would also be possible to miss out the section on practising vocabulary, as this is also dealt with in Unit 8.

A Warm-up

1 and 2

Allow the trainees a little time to think about the two questions before discussing them in groups and briefly reporting back to the class. Question 1 often elicits the answer 'phrase book' – this can be exploited to demonstrate that people instinctively value vocabulary linked by topic, and also 'chunks' of language which go beyond single words and have an immediate communicative value.

B Form, meaning and use

1 Ask the trainees to brainstorm all the information that they would expect to find about a word in a dictionary designed for language learners. Compare their ideas with those given below. Information about (a) the form consists of its spelling and pronunciation, (b) the meaning includes its definition (or 'denotation'), (c) the word's use includes its part of speech, grammatical information (countability, transitivity) and its style (e.g. informal).

Form	Meaning	Use
• spelling • phonemic transcriptions with stress patterns indicated	definitions or 'denotations' of words (You may wish to add that some words have 'connotations' – an evaluative element. *Arrogant* has a negative connotation whereas *self-confident* is more positive, for example.)	• part of speech, *e.g. noun* [C,U] • grammatical information, *e.g. transitive verb* • example sentences • information on formality

2 Knowing a word means correctly associating its form (either spoken or written), and its meaning. In addition, knowing how to use a word productively means knowing both the written and spoken forms of the word (i.e. its spelling and pronunciation); its meaning, including any connotations it has; its grammatical use, e.g. what part of speech it is, whether it is countable or uncountable, transitive or intransitive, etc.; its style or register, e.g. whether it is informal, technical, etc., and its typical environments, including the words it commonly co-occurs with (its collocations).

3 The teaching implications of the above might include:
- It is not enough to teach just the form of the word, or just its meaning.
- Teaching for production (i.e. speaking and writing) involves more steps than teaching simply for recognition.
- To teach all aspects of a word's form, meaning and use can be quite a lengthy process, so that, given the number of words that learners need, some of the work of vocabulary learning has to be entrusted to them, e.g. through extensive reading, learner training, etc.

C Learning about form and meaning

You may like to start by brainstorming different ways in which meaning could be conveyed. Translation is not covered in the examples but is an option when teaching a monolingual class. You could spend a few minutes discussing the advantages and disadvantages of using translation. It is quick and easy for the learners. It assumes that the teacher is fairly expert in both languages. It assumes that there is a direct equivalence between words in different languages, but this is not always the case.

1 You may prefer to demonstrate some or all of these techniques. Having read the lesson transcripts, trainees could work in small groups to complete the table and answer the questions. You may also want to comment on the fact that – in some of the extracts – the teacher attempts to elicit either the word or its meaning, perhaps assuming that some learners may already be familiar with it. (Eliciting is dealt with in more detail in Section D.)

	How is the meaning conveyed?	Is the spoken form practised?	How is the written form made clear?
a Beginners' class (1)	*by using pictures*	*Yes*	*The teacher writes it on the board.*
b Beginners' class (2)	*through demonstration*	*Yes*	*The teacher writes it on the board.*
c False beginners' class	*by using a picture*	*No*	*The teacher writes it on the board.*
d Elementary class	*with word relationships – in this case giving examples of 'co-hyponyms'*	*Yes*	*It is not dealt with.*
e Intermediate class	*with word relationships – a synonym in this case*	*It appears to be unnecessary as the learner said it appropriately.*	*The teacher writes it on the board.*
f Advanced class	*by giving a definition*	*It appears to be unnecessary as the learner said it appropriately.*	*It appears to already be in a text.*

2 1 Mime, demonstration, realia (real objects), etc.
   2 The teacher chooses to involve the rest of the group and addresses the question to them, before 'shaping' the answer volunteered, by using questions.
3 You could replace these words with ones that are likely to occur in teaching practice over the next few sessions. The trainees could work in groups to decide on the possible ways of teaching these words before reporting back to the class. There is no single correct answer, but some suggestions are given below. If you are short of time you could give one set of words to each group in the class, and then ask a spokesperson to report to the whole group.

Group 1: *pet*: by example: cats and dogs are types of pet, by explanation 'a domestic animal – one you keep in a house'.
to put down: by explanation 'to kill an animal for humane reasons because it is in pain'.
to vaccinate: by explanation 'to give a person or animal an injection to stop them getting a particular illness'.
Group 2: all of these could be presented using mime.
Group 3: all of these could be presented using realia or pictures.

Group 4: a combination of mime and explanation:
   punch – with a closed fist
   slap – with an open hand
   smack – with an open hand – usually as a punishment. In some cultures, a parent might smack a child.

D Eliciting vocabulary

1   Allow the trainees a few minutes to discuss their ideas before comparing in open class. The teacher elicits *pilot* but simply presents *doctor* and *nurse* – presumably because there is little chance of beginner students knowing the words. Generally eliciting is a useful technique. It may help the teacher to gauge the level of the class and will also involve learners more fully in the lesson. However, a teacher cannot elicit what is unknown to the group and must also have techniques for conveying meaning when the item is completely new to the learners.

2   Allow the trainees a few minutes to discuss their ideas in small groups before comparing with you.
   a   Not good advice: eliciting needs to be done quickly and efficiently or it will slow the lesson down too much. The prompts should be as transparent and as clear as possible.
   b   Good advice: finding the right prompt can be difficult for inexperienced teachers when they are under pressure in a lesson.
   c   Good advice: see above.
   d   Not good advice: you cannot elicit something which is unknown.
   e   Good advice: this often 'triggers' the word for learners.

3   You could replace these words with ones that are likely to occur in teaching practice over the next few sessions. Allow the trainees a few minutes to discuss their ideas in small groups before comparing with you.
   a   *watch* (noun): the teacher could point to his/her own watch and ask *What's this*?
   b   *game show*: through a definition: 'a type of television programme where ordinary people answer questions and do things to win prizes.' Or perhaps through examples, if there are suitable ones familiar to the whole group.
   c   *to flatter*: through a definition.
   d   *hurricane*: through a definition or through a picture.

E Checking understanding

1   Allow the trainees some time to discuss the techniques before discussing them in open class. You may wish to point out the following:
   a   Translation: fairly quick and in some ways efficient; it relies on the teacher having a fairly expert knowledge of both languages and also assumes that the class is monolingual. It may encourage learners to see words as having direct equivalents in other languages, whereas this is not always the case.
   b   *Do you understand?*: learners may be embarrassed about saying that they do not understand, or they may genuinely think that they do understand (in the case of 'false friends', for example) and therefore do not get the clarification they need.

   c Example sentence: this can be effective, as long as learners think of sentences that actually do give some demonstration of meaning. It is easy to think of sentences that do not demonstrate this. For example, 'The teacher just asked me to use the word *pogo* in a sentence.'

   d Short, easy to answer questions: can be useful as long as they are well designed and appropriate. See below for details.

2 a The teacher asks the questions in order to check understanding.

   b 1) No 2) Yes 3) No 4) Yes 5) No 6) Yes

   c The answers are all short and easy for the learners to give, if they understand the word being checked.

3 This could be done individually, with trainees checking with each other before checking with you.

Questions a and d are not useful. It may be worth highlighting at this point that good concept-checking questions are based on good language analysis. Trainees have to consider what could lead to misunderstanding and confusion and then focus questions on these areas.

4 Trainees could work in small groups to think about the language and to prepare appropriate questions.

Questions may vary, but sample ones are given below.

   a Do you use a briefcase for work or for holidays? (work) Do you put clothes in a briefcase? (no)

   b Would you say this to a friend? (yes) Would you write it in a job application? (no)

   c Was the car badly damaged or a bit damaged? (badly) Could it be repaired? (no)

   d Is there a coast between countries? (no) Do all countries have coasts? (no) Is the coast near the sea? (yes) Do people usually want to live on the coast? (yes – although there may be some cultural variation here)

   e Do you limp if you have hurt yourself? (yes) Do you limp if you are drunk? (no)

F Practising vocabulary

Allow the trainees to discuss the practice activities and answer the questions in small groups before reporting back. All the activities are intended as relevant and useful. The key point is that trainees appreciate the need to provide practice activities.

a Discussion:

   1 The level is flexible but learners need a degree of fluency – so pre-intermediate upwards.

   2 Not suitable for homework as it requires groups of learners and also monitoring by the teacher.

   3 Time allocation will depend on the level of the class. Higher level groups will probably be able to speak for longer.

   4 Speaking and listening are practised.

b Eliciting vocabulary:

   1 Depending on the words selected, this activity would be suitable for any level group.

   2 Not suitable for homework as it requires groups of learners and also monitoring by the teacher.

   3 The time required will depend on the number of words selected.

   4 Speaking and listening are practised.

c Gap-fill exercise:

   1 Suitable for all levels, and the 'clues' would need to be graded accordingly.

    2 Suitable for homework as learners can work individually.

    3 Time will depend on the number of examples.

    4 Reading and writing are practised.

G Classroom application: microteaching

Allow the groups time to prepare their teaching. Make sure that they understand that one person from each group will have to teach the rest of the class. Three possible groups of words are given below, but you may prefer to choose vocabulary that will come up in future teaching practice sessions.

Group 1	Group 2	Group 3
cousin	brake	stage
niece	accelerator	scenery
father-in-law	bonnet	to rehearse
to be engaged	to break down	script
to get divorced	to overtake	to be sold out

REFLECTION

Allow the trainees to work in groups to discuss their answers to the questions. When they have had some time to think about what happened and also to discuss it, conduct feedback with the whole class.

You could close the lesson by using the optional activity.

Optional activity

Select a vocabulary activity from a current coursebook. Ensure that there are enough copies for trainees to work in groups of two or three. Ask the trainees to analyse the material and answer the following questions.

1 How is form dealt with?

2 How is meaning dealt with?

3 Is information given about how the words are used?

4 How much practice is provided?

5 Can you think of ways of adapting or extending this material?

6 Presenting grammar (1)

Main focus
Ways of presenting grammar.

Learning outcomes
- Trainees understand the basic principles of conveying the meaning of new grammatical patterns.
- Trainees understand the basic principles of highlighting the form of new grammatical patterns.

Key concepts
- conveying meaning
- highlighting form; modeling, model sentence
- guided discovery; inductive presentation

Stage	Focus
A Warm-up	introducing the topic
B Three presentations	comparing and contrasting three approaches to presentation
C Conveying the meaning of a grammar item	exploring different ways of presenting meaning
D Highlighting the form of a new grammar item	introducing ways of highlighting the spoken and written form of a new grammar item
Reflection	trainees reflect on what they have learned

A Warm-up

Allow the trainees a little time to think about the questions before discussing them in small groups. When they have had sufficient time, ask the groups to report back to the class.

1 There are parallels between learning grammar and other new skills. The language teacher can also tell people about grammar. Learners can be shown how grammar is used in context. Learners can read about grammar for themselves in reference books. Learners can try communicating using the language they have and pick up grammar as they go along. Of course, learners may chop and change between preferred strategies.

2 Answers may vary, but it could be argued that the processes are similar and therefore the strategies may well be similar.

B Three presentations

1 Tell the trainees that you are going to demonstrate three short lessons at an elementary level, and explain that the trainees themselves will take the role of the learners.

2 The demonstration lessons should follow the spirit if not the letter of these scripts:

Demonstration lesson 1:

Teacher: When we want to talk about our future plans, we can use the form *going to*. For example, *Next weekend I am going to play football.* [Teacher writes this sentence on the board.] Can you repeat that? [Class repeats.] Or, *This evening I am going to phone my sister.* Everybody. [Class repeats.] Or, *Next winter I'm going to learn to ski.* These are my plans. You use *going to* with the infinitive: *going to play, going to phone, going to learn.* So, what are *you* going to do next weekend? [Teacher asks individual students.]

Demonstration lesson 2:

Teacher: OK, everyone. Listen and watch me. It's hot in here. *I'm going to open the window.* [Walks to the window and opens it.] OK. But it's very noisy. *I'm going to close the window.* [Closes it.] OK, now *I'm going to open the door.* [Walks to the door and opens it.] OK. Now it's time for the lesson. *I'm going to write on the board.* What was the first sentence I said? [Writes the sentences that have been previously presented, and highlights the form and meaning of *going to*.]

Demonstration lesson 3:

Teacher: [Draws person's face on board.] OK, this is Jo. [Draws thought bubble above the face.] Jo's thinking about the future. [Draws plane in thought bubble.] He's thinking about his next holiday. What's he going to do? [Draws Eiffel Tower in thought bubble; elicits *He's going to fly to Paris.*] Everybody, repeat. *He's going to fly to Paris.* [Class repeats; teacher draws ticket in Jo's hand.] Has he got the ticket? [Students: Yes.] So, is he deciding to go to Paris now, or did he decide before? [Students: Before.] So, this is Jo's plan. Where's he going to stay? [Teacher draws a smiling face in the thought bubble.] Listen, *He's going to stay with a friend.* Everybody. [Class repeats.] He's planned this already. What's he going to do in Paris? What's he going to see? What's he going to eat? [Teacher elicits possible responses, and drills these; all the sentences that have been drilled are then re-elicited and written on the board. The teacher highlights the form and meaning of *going to*.]

'Teach' the three lessons consecutively, making it clear where one finishes and the next begins. Then allow trainees time to compare their reactions and feelings in pairs or small groups.

2 The expected answer to this question is: (1) explanation; (2) demonstration; (3) situation. There is clearly some overlap here since lessons (2) and (3) both involve some explanation too, but that is not their starting point, nor their main focus. Allow some time to discuss the pros and cons of the three different approaches. It is expected that trainees will prefer the more interactive and involving, and the less wordy, presentations 2 and 3, but it is worth pointing out that sometimes explanation can be an appropriate and effective vehicle of presentation, e.g. when dealing with grammar issues that arise in the course of other activities, but always assuming learners have the metalanguage to cope with it.

C Conveying the meaning of a grammar item

1 Review the ways that meaning was conveyed in the presentations 2 and 3 in the previous activity, and highlight the usefulness of visual means of presentation. Allow trainees to work together to suggest uses for the visuals. Possible structures that could be taught using these pictures include:
- *needs doing* (*It needs painting.*)
- *present perfect* – for present results (*They've painted the windows.*)

- *present perfect passive* (*The windows have been fixed.*)
- causative *have* (*They had the windows fixed.*)
- *used to* (*The garden used to be a mess.*)
- comparatives (*The garden is tidier; The house is cleaner.*)

As an option, you may like to ask trainees to plan the stages of a presentation based on these pictures. You could also bring in other pictures that suggest particular structures, e.g. making deductions about the scene of a crime using *must/could/might have…*

2 You may like to assign different structures to different groups. Point out that trainees don't have to fill in every cell in the table. Possible answers are:

Grammar item	Demonstration	Visual aids	Situation
can/can't (for ability)	Ask learners to perform actions in the class, some of which are possible, and others not, e.g. Touch the ceiling (to elicit: *I can't …*); Open the door …(*I can …*), etc.	Pictures of animals, to elicit *A cheetah can run fast; a bat can't see very well; a kangaroo can jump …* etc.	Interview for a job requiring lots of skills, e.g. au pair: *Can you drive? Can you cook?* etc.
used to (for past habits)		Picture of person before and after radical cosmetic surgery: *He used to have big ears … etc.*	Story of person who has experienced a major lifestyle change, by, for example, winning a lottery, or marrying into royalty, or downsizing
present continuous (for activities happening at the moment of speaking)	Perform action such as walking, sitting, opening doors, etc. and say what you are doing as you do them	Wall chart with lots of activities happening simultaneously, e.g. party, beach or street scene	Two people communicating by mobile phone, reporting on what their family members are doing at the moment
must have done (for making deductions about past situations)		Scene of crime picture: *They must have come in through the bathroom window …*	mysterious situation, such as the *Mary Celeste* (ship found abandoned on the high seas)

3 Trainees will be continuing to work on their presentations in the next activity.

D Highlighting the form of a new grammar item

Allow time for trainees to read through the transcript silently. Alternatively, assign roles to different individuals who read the transcript aloud.

1 The teacher conveys the meaning in turn a (using a situation); the teacher highlights the spoken form in turn c, and the written form in turns k and m.

2 1 The teacher is asking concept questions in order to highlight the concept of high probability, but not certainty.

   2 Possibly because the teacher believes that exposure to the written form might interfere with the pronunciation of the structure; or possibly because it is easier to maintain the learners' attention by focusing on the spoken form initially and discouraging writing.

   3 The teacher is directing attention on to the rules of form, and making these explicit, perhaps in the belief that implicit learning leaves too much to chance.

3 Allow trainees, working in groups, to fine-tune their presentation ideas from the last activity, so that they include at least these three stages:
   • presentation of meaning (including checking of understanding of concept)
   • highlighting of spoken form
   • highlighting of written form, including rule(s) of form

As a further activity, trainees could jointly plan presentations that are forthcoming in their TP classes.

REFLECTION

Presenting new language items	
DOs	DON'Ts
• Involve learners in the process as much as possible. • Check that learners have understood the meaning. • Highlight the form. • Remember that different learners may have different preferences for how new language items are presented.	• Give a lecture about grammar. • Always use the same presentation technique.

7 Presenting grammar (2)

Main focus

Ways of presenting grammar: checking understanding and providing controlled practice.

Learning outcomes

- Trainees are introduced to ways of checking the meaning of new grammatical patterns.
- Trainees are introduced to the use of timelines.
- Trainees are introduced to ways of providing practice of new grammatical patterns.

Key concepts

- checking understanding: concept questions
- timelines
- controlled/restricted practice

Stage	Focus
A Warm-up	review of words relating to the teaching of grammar
B Checking understanding	introducing ways of checking understanding of new grammar
C Timelines	introducing the use of timelines
D Ways of practising grammar	introducing ways of practising language in a restricted context
E Planning a grammar lesson	sequencing the elements of a grammar presentation
Reflection	trainees reflect on what they have learned

There is one optional activity that supports the unit, in which trainees select and analyse part of a grammar lesson taken from the internet.

A Warm-up

Start the activity by writing on the board *A good grammar presentation should …* and elicit a way of continuing the sentence. Then ask the trainees to work together to produce more sentences. Possible sentences might be: *A good grammar presentation should be clear/memorable/economical; … should build on what the learners already know; … should include a focus on form and a focus on meaning …; … should include a statement of the rule … .* etc. Ask groups to report back in open class, and challenge them to justify their criteria, by asking *why*? (Note that this format can be used to review many of the sessions.)

B Checking understanding

1 You may like to review what trainees remember of checking the understanding of vocabulary before moving on to this. This may help to make this section less daunting. Allow the trainees to spend some time looking at the techniques individually before discussing their ideas in pairs.

   a Not a very useful technique. Some learners may think that they understand, when in fact they don't. Others may be embarrassed to say that they do not understand in front of the whole class.

   b The repetition of the new item of language (*used to*) in the question makes this unreliable. It could be compared to asking, 'Is a duck a duck?'

   c This may be useful in some circumstances, as long as the teacher has a good knowledge of both languages. However, it may encourage learners to see grammar patterns as having direct equivalents in different languages, and this may not always be the case. It obviously cannot work in a multilingual class.

   d Useful: this approach is further developed in the following part of this section.

   e Useful: you may like to point out that asking concept-checking questions is not the only way to check learner understanding.

2 Ensure that trainees understand that they do not need to check the meaning of the lexis. So, they do not check the meaning of 'break up' for example, but of the past perfect. Answers will vary but example questions are given below.

   a Am I on the plane now? (no)
     Is it likely that I have booked my ticket already? (yes)
     Is this about the present or the future? (future)

   b What happened first? I met her or she broke up with Chris? (broke up with Chris)

   c Am I Prime Minister? (no)
     Is it likely that I will be Prime Minister? (no)
     Is this about the past or present/future time? (present/future)

C Timelines

You may want to spend a little time explaining the particular conventions that you would like trainees to use.

1 Allow the trainees to work together in pairs to try to match the timelines to the pictures. Conduct feedback and clarify any points that they are unsure of. Point out how a state is represented differently to a repeated action.

   Answers: a–iv; b–iii; c–ii; d–i

2 Conventions of drawing timelines may vary but below are possible answers.

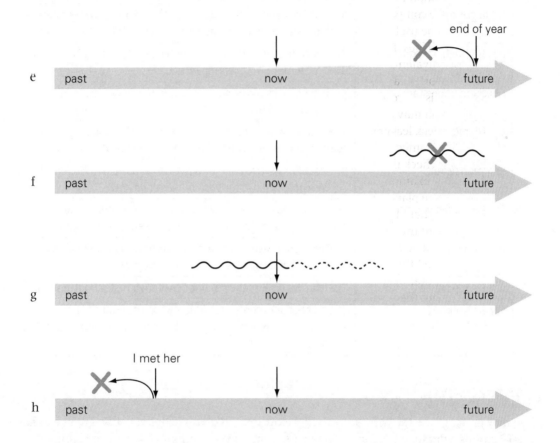

D Ways of practising grammar

Allow the trainees to discuss the material in small groups before reporting back to the class. You may wish to point out:

1 3.3 personalises the language use. 4 contrasts the two forms.
2 3.1 and 3.2 appear to be fairly form-focused. In 4, the emphasis is on meaning.
3 3.1, 3.2 and 3.3 all involve oral production. 4 is comprehension-based, and involves reading.

E Planning a grammar lesson

The trainees could work together to piece together the lesson plan. You may like to stress that this is one model for a lesson plan, and is not the only way that grammar teaching could be approached.

Stage	Procedure
Building context	1e The class talks about what things they enjoyed doing when they were children.
2h Model sentence	Teacher says *David used to play football*.
Highlight meaning	3a The teacher draws a timeline on the board, showing a period in the past with several crosses within it.
4b Highlight spoken form	The teacher repeats the model sentence with natural linking, stress and intonation. The class repeats.
Checking understanding	5j Teacher asks *Did he play football in the past?* (Yes) *Does he play football now?* (No)
6c Highlight written form	The teacher writes the model sentence on the board. Draws a box round 'used to' and writes 'base form' over 'play'.
Summarise 'rule'	7f Teacher says *Used to + infinitive can be used to talk about things we regularly did in the past, but don't do now.*
8i Restricted practice	Learners choose an activity they enjoyed as children and then walk round the class asking if other people used to do the same thing.
Report back	9d The teacher asks some individuals how many people shared their interest and corrects errors if they are made.
10g Freer practice	The learners discuss their memories of their first school in small groups.
Report back	The teacher asks some individuals what they talked about. Afterwards she writes some errors she heard on the board and asks learners to correct them.

REFLECTION

You may prefer to use the optional activity below instead of this activity. You might like to have the TP groups work together for this activity so that they are thinking of the same group of learners. You may like to select appropriate grammar sections for them to look at.

Allow each group time to consider the material and the questions asked. You could get a member from each group to join with members of other groups to explain the material they have looked at and how they think it could be adapted, before reporting back.

Optional activity

Ask the trainees to search the internet for a grammar lesson that they feel would be relevant for the class they are teaching. They should then print off the lesson and analyse it, using the questions in the Reflection activity. They should pay particular attention to areas that would need to be adapted.

8 Practising new language

Main focus

Controlled (or restricted) practice of new language.

Learning outcomes

- Trainees are introduced to ways of practising the meaning and form of new language in controlled (or restricted) contexts.
- Trainees are introduced to ideas of how to select and sequence activities according to the needs of a group.

Key concepts

- repetition; choral and individual drills
- accuracy vs fluency
- interactive and communicative practice
- dialogues
- personalisation

Stage	Focus
A Warm-up	introducing the topic
B Practice drills	introducing the rationale and mechanics of drilling
C Written practice	introducing common types of controlled written practice
D Interactive and communicative practice	introducing the principles of interactive and communicative practice activities
E Dialogue building	introducing the stages of dialogue building
Reflection	trainees reflect on what they have learned

There are two optional activities to support the unit.
Optional activity 1: trainees analyse some published ELT material.
Optional activity 2: trainees practise dialogue building.

A Warm-up

If you prefer, you could start the session with books closed and discuss different learning experiences and their parallels with language learning.

Allow the trainees to read the two short texts and encourage them to discuss the parallels with language learning in small groups. Remind them to discuss their own experiences.

The tennis example highlights practising parts of something in isolation and repeatedly before attempting to integrate the new skill into existing skills.

The cooking example takes a far more 'deep-end' approach, with the learner experimenting, benefiting from guidance (including both positive and negative feedback), but essentially learning in a more holistic sense.

B Practice drills

Using the trainees as students, demonstrate a short lesson sequence (about 5–10 minutes at most) that includes the introduction of some vocabulary items and a structure, or idiomatic (multi-word) expression. Ideally the lesson should be in a language that the learners are not familiar with, but if this is not possible, the lesson can be in English. The lesson should include examples of the teacher modelling and choral drilling the new language items, followed by individual drilling and correction. For example:

Teacher: Listen. She's been to Spain. She's been to Spain. Now you. Repeat.
Class: She's been to Spain.
Teacher: Good. Cinzia, can you say it?
Cinzia: She has been to Spain.
Teacher: OK – but put 'she' and 'has' together. Try again.
Cinzia: She's been to Spain.
Teacher: Great. Roberto …

At the conclusion of the lesson, ask the learners to discuss the questions 1–6, and then to report back. The following points could be made:

- Drilling was originally devised as a way of forming good language 'habits', and as a focus on accuracy. More recently, drilling is justified as a way of fixing formulaic chunks in working memory, and/or as a way of practising oral fluidity, including the appropriate use of stress, rhythm and intonation.
- Not all new language items may need to be drilled. Drilling is useful if learners have problems articulating the new item, e.g. if they find it difficult to produce the elements of the structure in a fluid manner. It may also be a useful in aiding the memorisation of formulaic language, such as common sentence stems (*Would you like … Have you ever … ?* etc.).

The pros of drilling include: it gives the learners initial confidence, and choral drills allow them to 'have a go' without feeling conspicuous; repetition can aid memory; it serves to highlight the key language items in a lesson. The cons include: it can become mindless 'parroting', if overdone, and it can have an infantilising effect, which may not be appropriate for older learners; repetition is no guarantee that new language items are stored in long-term memory.

C Written practice

1 The activities become increasingly challenging. In (a) the actual words are supplied in the correct form. In (b) the verbs are supplied but the correct forms have to be inserted, and in (c) the learner has to think of an appropriate verb (there are several possibilities in most cases) and then put it into the correct form. This sort of exercise can be easily manipulated to suit the learning needs of a class, or indeed, individuals within a class.

2 The activities are different from drills in that: (fairly obviously) they are written and not spoken; they don't involve repetition; they require the learners to make choices and display knowledge about the form and/or meaning of the target language items. The advantages of using written exercises are: learners can work at their own pace and/or in pairs; it is easier for the teacher to monitor each learner's progress; it is perhaps easier for learners to focus on the formal features of the new language items.

3   The activity is less controlled in that it requires learners to produce larger stretches of language and there is no single correct answer. Activities such as these can be useful in consolidating learning, for example, as a homework task. In a lesson they can help to provide a change of pace and energy. They also may be successfully used before oral practice as they allow more thinking time and learners can get their 'minds around' the new item without the added pressure of getting their 'tongues around' it. This may be particularly true for complex structures (such as this one), or for items of language that are more common in written than spoken language, such as some aspects of reported speech or the use of passive forms.

4   You may decide to choose a language focus that is related to a forthcoming teaching practice point. Trainees should work in pairs or small groups: they need only design three or four items for each exercise.

D   Interactive and communicative practice

1   Again, you may like to briefly demonstrate some of the activities in this section or the following sections. Trainees may have a better idea of the 'mechanics' of an activity from having experienced it than from having read a description of it and will also find it more engaging.

Do one example with the class first. It is important to establish the difference between an activity that is simply interactive, i.e. one where learners interact and/or take turns; and one that is communicative, i.e. one in which the outcome of the activity depends on the learners listening to one another and processing what they hear. In the latter, learners will need to negotiate and repair communication breakdowns, and adapt their own contributions in accordance with their partner's: there is an element of unpredictability.

	A Dialogue practice	B Circle drill	C Spot the difference	D Find someone who	E Writing sentences
There is built-in repetition: the activity gives learners opportunities to use the new language item on several occasions.	✓	✓	✓	✓	✓
The language is contextualised.	✓		✓		
Learners interact and/or take turns.	✓	✓	✓	✓	✓
Learners communicate – they must both speak and listen to what is said.			✓	✓	✓
The language is personalised.		✓		✓	✓
The activity is fun and playful*.		✓	✓	✓	

* This is subjective to some extent.

2 Initiate a discussion on the advantages of activities that have one or more of these characteristics. (Note that none of the example activities has *all* these characteristics – that would be a tall order.) Points that may come up include the following:

a repetition: the acquisition of a new skill usually involves some element of repetition: why should language be different?

b context: this helps reinforce the meaning of the new item, and shows how it might be used in real life.

c interaction: most authentic language use is interactive in some way; learners can work together and maximise learning and practice opportunities.

d communication: the ability to negotiate and repair communication breakdown, and to adapt one's message according to the ongoing nature of the discourse is crucial for effective real-life communication.

e personalisation: language practice is likely to be more interesting and hence more memorable if it is personalised.

f fun: activities are often more motivating if there is a fun element.

You could use optional activity 1 at this point.

REFLECTION

Allow the trainees to think individually for a few moments about the questions, and then encourage them to share their ideas in small groups. You may like to highlight the following points.

a Knowing a rule – in the sense of being able to put it into words – is different to being able to operate it under time pressure, which typically applies when speaking, for example. Spoken practice of new language items should help to make the use of those items more automatic and therefore make language production more fluent.

b As these activities are partly targeted at promoting accuracy, then in most cases teachers would probably want to correct learners as they go along. Also, by correcting learners from time to time, the teacher is gently reminding the learners that they should pay at least some attention to form.

c The activities in this unit have all been fairly controlled. Learners will also need to practise with fluency-focused activities. (See Unit B13.)

d Not necessarily. It is often assumed that there is a progression from 'controlled' to 'freer' activities within a lesson but this need not always be the case. However, the notion of 'controlled' is not unproblematic in itself because activities may be controlled either in the sense that the teacher controls who says what, and when they should say it, or in the sense that there is tight control over the language used in the activity. Drills, for example are controlled in both senses, but a Find Someone Who … exercise is only controlled in the latter sense. There is no reason why the teacher shouldn't sometimes challenge the learners early on with an activity which is relatively free and then go back to something more restricted if it is necessary. Activities need to be sequenced in accordance with the needs and preferences of the group. The key thing is for teachers to be able to provide a lot of varied practice activities.

Optional activity 1

Select some coursebook presentations of new items of language and ask the trainees to analyse them using the criteria in Section D in the Trainee Book.

Optional activity 2

Dialogue building

Trainees work in small groups. Give them an item of language. You could use any item of language for this exercise. Functional language (such as making suggestions, requests and so on) would work well. Again, you may like to use a language item that will soon be taught in their teaching practice. Each group should:

a think of a context in which the item of language could be used
b write a short dialogue that includes the language item at least once
c elicit their dialogue from the rest of the class, ensuring there is some choral and individual repetition of parts
d set up some pairwork to practise the dialogue

9 Error correction

Main focus	Key concepts
Ways of correcting errors.	• errors, mistakes
Learning outcomes	• correction: teacher, peer, self
• Trainees understand the principal considerations in dealing with errors.	• reformulation
• Trainees learn a variety of techniques for dealing with errors.	• immediate vs delayed correction

Stage	Focus
A Warm-up	introducing some background views on error
B Types of error	introducing trainees to types of error
C When to correct	introducing some of the principal considerations in deciding when it is appropriate to correct
D Correction strategies	introducing correction strategies
E Demonstration	the trainer demonstrates some correction techniques
F Classroom application	trainees practise different correction techniques
Reflection	trainees put what they have learned into practice

Note: The term 'error' is used throughout this unit. The literature on error often draws a distinction between mistakes, which are not systematic, and 'errors', which are systematic, i.e. they are evidence of the learner's developing language system, or 'interlanguage'. In theory, a learner can self-correct a mistake because they know the correct form – they simply 'got it wrong' on one occasion, perhaps through inattention and the demands of 'on-line' processing. However, a learner might not be able to self-correct an error since it results from a gap in their knowledge. In practice, it is difficult, if not impossible, for the teacher to decide if a non-standard form is systematic or non-systematic, so the distinction is ignored in this unit.

Dealing with errors in written work is dealt with in Unit 14.

A Warm-up

1 Allow the trainees some time to discuss the different teachers' approaches in small groups before reporting back to the whole class.
Avoiding error is very difficult if learners are given any freedom to create the messages they want to with the language. Most people would argue that learners should be encouraged to become 'risk-takers' and this will inevitably lead to some errors, which is largely Mariagrazia's position. Over-correction may lead to a loss of confidence (Paula) but it is

worth pointing out to trainees that the majority of learners expect their teacher to correct them and are far more likely to complain if they are never corrected than if they are corrected a lot. Error correction should, of course, be done in a sensitive and encouraging way.

B Types of error

We suggest that you collect some errors made by learners in TP sessions before you do this unit. Collecting these errors could be part of an observation task for trainees, and then they could be analysed in activity B2.

1 This should be quite easy. The aim is simply to demonstrate that not all errors are grammar errors. In fact, errors in vocabulary and prosodic features of pronunciation may lead to more breakdowns in communication than many grammar errors. Of course, this activity does not cover all possible categories of error.

Allow the trainees some time to complete the matching activity individually before checking with a partner and then confirming those answers in open class.

The answers are:

1–f)–present perfect would be more appropriate.

2–e)–too informal for the given context.

3–d)–*injured* or *hurt* rather than *damaged* (which is not used to describe people).

4–b)

5–a)

6–c)

C When to correct

Allow the trainees some time to discuss the situations in pairs before they report back. Arguments could be made for alternative strategies, so there is no single correct answer, but some suggestions follow:

Lesson 1: (Note: only two speakers have made errors.) The learners are communicating and there seems little point in disrupting the flow of the lesson with immediate correction. However, higher-level learners are often fluent and need to work on becoming more accurate, and so some delayed correction may be appropriate. You might like to point out that at lower levels a teacher may choose to correct less often, in the interests of encouraging learners to keep talking.

Lesson 2: The learner's message is very unclear and so communication breaks down. When this happens, meaning needs to be 'negotiated', usually by asking questions – a form of immediate correction.

Lesson 3: It would be inappropriate to correct the learner when the focus is a social or interpersonal one.

Lesson 4: The teacher's aim is to check comprehension of a listening task. As long as meaning is clear (and assuming *saxophone* is the correct answer) it may prove distracting to correct small grammar lapses. However, the teacher may choose to reformulate the answer by saying something like: *Yes, that's right. He plays the saxophone.*

D Correction strategies

1 Give the trainees some time to look at the responses in pairs before conducting a group discussion and highlighting the key points.

a The teacher tries to prompt the learner to self-correct. The value of encouraging self-correction before peer- or teacher-correction could be discussed at this point.

b The teacher repeats the learner's utterance up to the point of the error, in order to elicit a self-correction.

c Using fingers (called finger correction) in this way can be useful in focusing learners on exactly where the error occurred, again, as a prompt for self-correction.

d The teacher asks a question to establish the learner's intended meaning. By implying that the message was not clear, the teacher may be encouraging the learner to re-think the way the message was formulated – a further way of encouraging self-correction.

e The teacher reformulates (or recasts) the learner's utterance. However, the learner may not realise she is being corrected. Often such reformulations go unnoticed by learners. On the other hand it allows the flow of the lesson to continue.

f The teacher has decided not to interrupt the activity flow, but to note errors as they occur, and then go back to them at the end of the activity.

2 Ask trainees to reflect on the correction strategies they have seen, either in their teaching practice, or in their observed classes. If you have access to video or DVD footage of classes in progress, these can be a useful way of showing different correction strategies in action, and of evaluating their effectiveness.

3 If you are short of time, you may like to divide the class into pairs and ask each pair just to look at one or two strategies, before they report back.

Correction strategy	Advantages	Disadvantages
a Teacher prompts using terminology, e.g. 'grammar', 'tense', 'pronunciation', etc.	Easy to use. Indicates the type of error that the learner should be looking for.	Learners need to be familiar with the terminology used.
b Teacher repeats the utterance to the point of the error, e.g. *Yesterday you …*	Quick and easy. Gives guidance as to where exactly the problem is.	Teacher needs to use appropriate intonation, or gesture, to ensure that the learner understands that this is a correction procedure and not part of the communication.
c Finger correction	Gives a very clear indication of where the problem is. Quite flexible – can be used to indicate the need to put a word in, take a word out, run words together ('I'm' etc.).	Only works with short utterances. Takes practice for most teachers to become confident.

Correction strategy	Advantages	Disadvantages
d Teacher uses questions, e.g. *Do you mean you go every day?*	A good way to discover the learner's intended message and 'repairs' the communication after a breakdown.	Questions need to be clear and easy to answer to avoid further confusing the learner.
e Reformulation, e.g. *You went to the beach.*	Quick and easy. Doesn't break the flow of communication.	Learners may not realise that they are being corrected and it may therefore have little impact.
f Delayed correction	Does not interfere with the flow of communication. The teacher has time to prepare what to say, rather than having to do it immediately.	Correction has less impact if 'served cold'.

E Demonstration

1 Ask the trainees to close their books so that they do not try to complete the table as you go along. Give out the grey cards to a selection of trainees. Tell the trainees that they should say **exactly** what is on the card, i.e. they should not produce a corrected version.
Correct the errors in any way in which you feel comfortable – it would be useful to demonstrate a range of techniques, including some from the previous section.

Her father is a **PRO**fessor.	Bring me the menu!	My brother fell off his bike but he wasn't badly damaged.
Can you borrow me some money?	Do you can juggle?	Where is going Felipe?

© Cambridge University Press 2007

2 Ask the trainees to open their books and allow them to work in groups to complete the table.

F Classroom application

Ensure that the trainees understand the instruction in their books. Give each group a set of cards.

When the trainees have had time to practise, collect in the cards, nominate a trainee, read out one of the cards and let the trainee correct you.

He likes CIGars.

I have tree sisters.

(said with very flat, 'bored' intonation) I can't wait for the next session.

(in a bar and to a member of the bar staff...)
I want a beer.

She no likes me anymore.

Helen is wedding her boyfriend next week.

Do we must leave now?

I leaving here on Friday.

Paula and Chris is married for two years.

He stopped to smoke three years ago.

He has brother.

I had gone to cinema yesterday.

I was late because I stopped talking to a friend.

She likes her job. She works for the same company for years.

I going to New York at the weekend.

© Cambridge University Press 2007

Encourage trainees to discuss what they consider to be the main things they have learned about correction before filling in the mind map. Stress that they can add bubbles as they wish and need not feel constrained by what is on the page in front of them. Allow some time for them to compare their completed maps with other pairs before briefly reporting back their ideas to the class.

Trainees may include: types of error (problems with word stress, intonation, word order, choice of words, register, verb forms and so on) and strategies for correcting errors (including such things as: using terminology, repeating the utterance to the point of the error, using fingers, asking questions, delayed correction and so on).

10 Developing listening skills

Main focus
To learn the basic principles of developing the listening skill, and to apply these to the design of a skills-based lesson.

Learning outcomes
- Trainees understand different purposes and ways of listening.
- Trainees understand how top-down and bottom-up factors influence comprehension.
- Trainees can apply these understandings to the development of the listening skill.

Key concepts
- interactive/non-interactive listening
- transactional listening, listening for pleasure
- listening for gist, intensive listening
- top-down vs bottom-up processing
- pre-listening, while-listening and post-listening tasks

Stage	Focus
A Warm-up	reflecting on real-life listening, and categorising listening events
B Comprehension	distinguishing between top-down (knowledge-based) and bottom-up (language-based) factors in understanding
C Listening texts and tasks	matching text and task
D A listening lesson	identifying the aims and sequencing principles of the stages of a listening lesson
E Classroom application	applying these principles to the design of a listening lesson
Reflection	reflecting on some of the problems faced by learners and teacher in classroom listening activities

A Warm-up

1 Start the activity by giving some examples of your own – including examples that involved both speaking and listening.
2 Point out that each listening experience may involve more than one item from the list a–f. In the discussion, the following points should be highlighted:
   - Listening can range from being very interactive to wholly non-interactive.
   - Listening can be face-to-face, or 'disembodied', as when listening to the radio or on the phone; it can also be reinforced with images, as when watching a film or TV.
   - The purposes of listening can vary, from the purely transactional (as when information is being conveyed) to 'listening for pleasure', as when listening to songs, or when watching a film.
   - Listening can be intensive, where every word counts, or it can involve simply listening to the gist.

3 All of these situations present possible difficulties, exacerbated by the fact that the listener is not a native speaker. Factors that could make listening difficult include:

- the lack of visual reinforcement, as when listening to the radio or when on the phone (although sometimes the visual reinforcement can be distracting)
- the inability to interact, in order to negotiate breakdowns in communication, as when listening to the radio or TV
- the inability to control the rate of the input, by 'pausing' or 'replaying' it, as is possible when a text is recorded
- the pressure, in face-to-face interaction, to speak, which might interfere with listening
- poor acoustics, as in many classrooms
- the topic, e.g. the news may be more difficult than a song, because of the density of information, lack of repetition, etc.; on the other hand, song lyrics are often idiomatic, elliptical, and hard to hear.

B Comprehension

1 Read the following two texts to the trainees, at a natural speed, with natural pausing. Avoid supplying any paralinguistic support, e.g. the use of gesture, in order to clarify understanding. Allow the trainees to discuss their level of understanding. If requested, read the texts again.

Text a[1]:

Before they start, conditions are less than ideal and security is at risk. But the problem is soon resolved as each of their adjacent arms repeatedly describes the same short arc, the one in time with the other. In this way the impediment is removed, thus avoiding the need to stop and perform the operation by hand. The process continues until such time as a change in conditions renders it unnecessary.

Text b[1]:

We sat down at the table in the corner and the forby took our order. To start with, Therese ordered gumble, and I had a green dibblet. For the main course, Therese went for the pan-fried lunk with a fibitch sauce, while I opted for the house speciality, a shoulder of roast chorton. We washed all this down with a bottle of their best white jimmery.

---

2 Read these second versions of the texts (the differences are in italics):

Text a[2]:

Windscreen wipers.

Before they start, conditions are less than ideal and security is at risk. But the problem is soon resolved as each of their adjacent arms repeatedly describes the same short arc, the one in time with the other. In this way the impediment is removed, thus avoiding the need to stop and perform the operation by hand. The process continues until such time as a change in conditions renders it unnecessary.

Text b[2]:

We sat down at the table in the corner and the *waiter* took our order. To start with, Therese ordered *soup*, and I had a green *salad*. For the main course, Therese went for the pan-fried *sole* with a *dill* sauce, while I opted for the house speciality, a shoulder of roast *lamb*. We washed all this down with a bottle of their best white *wine*.

In discussing the task, the following points should be noted:

1) and 2) Comprehension depends on a number of factors, and is not simply a case of 'understanding every word'. In the first text (in its first version), trainees will have understood all the words, but will probably have been unsure as to what the text was about. They lacked the necessary (extralinguistic) background information to make sense of the words. In other words, they lacked *top-down knowledge*.

In the second text (in its first version), they were unfamiliar with a number of the words (because they were invented): they lacked some *bottom-up knowledge*. But they had a clear idea of the situation, and therefore could supply some of the missing (linguistic) information. Comprehension, then, results from the interaction of top-down and bottom-up levels of knowledge.

This is true for both reading and listening. (Reading is dealt with in Unit 11.)

3) and 4) The implications are that in order to maximise comprehension, it helps:

- to establish the general situation, topic, context, etc. of the text (to activate top-down knowledge)
- to provide help with individual words (bottom-up knowledge), e.g. in the form of pre-teaching, or allowing dictionary use

When choosing or designing listening texts, these factors can be balanced against one another, in order to achieve an appropriate level of difficulty.

C Listening texts and tasks

1 Appropriate tasks for each of these text types might include:
1 a news broadcast: *a, c, g*
2 the directions to a person's home: *d, g*
3 the description of a missing person: *f, j*
4 an embarrassing personal anecdote: *a, b*
5 a shopping dialogue (sales assistant and customer): *a*
6 a pop song: *a, f, h, i, k*
7 recorded entertainment information (e.g. movies, theatre, etc.): *a, e, g*
8 a weather forecast: *a, d, e, h*

2 Criteria for choosing a task include:
- Does the task replicate an authentic (i.e. 'real-life') response to the material? For example, when listening to directions, we often take notes and/or draw a rough map.
- Does the task reflect the way the information is organised? For example, information that is in a particular sequence (as in a story) is best extracted by means of a sequencing task; on the other hand, information which is organised into categories (such as entertainment information) is best extracted by means of a grid or table.

Note that the most generally applicable task type is *a* (answering *wh*-questions): most listening texts lend themselves to this treatment. On the other hand, the least applicable task types are *i* and *k*, (writing the exact words or filling in gaps), since these do not usually reflect real-life listening tasks. However, they can be useful in the classroom in order to focus on specific language features in a text, but may be best used *after* tasks that require less intensive listening.

D A listening lesson

1   Activity 1a: (*pre-listening*): activating interest and background knowledge; pre-teaching vocabulary.
Activity 1b: (*while-listening*): gist listening; gaining overall familiarity with content.
Activity 2a: more detailed check of understanding, leading to second listening (*re-listening*).
Activity 3a: using transcript to match spoken and written texts, and to help resolve problems of understanding (*re-listening*); focus on a discrete feature of the spoken text (sentence stress: *post-listening*).
Activity 3b: application of discrete feature (*post-listening*).
Activity 3c: checking (*re-listening*).

2   It may be worth pointing out that there is no single correct order, but that the ordering of stages will follow a logic dictated in part by the content of the text, the level of the class, and the purpose of the activity. Nevertheless, a basic 'default' order might be: d), e), f), b), c), a).

3   The rationale for this order is:
d   Activating interest and background (top-down) knowledge helps understanding.
e   Pre-teaching vocabulary (bottom-up knowledge) helps understanding.
f   Setting a task provides a motivation to listen; more general tasks precede more specific tasks.
b   More specific tasks, requiring more intensive listening, follow more extensive tasks.
c   Following the transcript helps resolve residual problems of understanding, and forms links between aural signal and written words.
a   The text is used as a source of language focus, but only after it has been thoroughly understood.

E Classroom application

1   Point out that this three-way division is a convenient way of classifying listening (and reading) tasks. Pre-listening: *d, e*; while-listening: *f, b, c*; post-listening: *a*.

2   Trainees work in small groups, and should be prepared to present their tasks to the class. It is expected that their task sequences should reflect the principles outlined above.
(Note: As an alternative, set the trainees a text from the current coursebook they are using, in the form of the transcript; they can then compare their treatment of the text with the way it is dealt with in the coursebook. Different groups can also work with different texts.)

REFLECTION

Points that could be made include:
Q1: Speaking *involves* listening, so for learners who want to learn to speak, listening would seem to be essential; also, there are some grounds to believe that 'understanding messages' is a prerequisite for language acquisition.
Q2: There are acceptable alternatives, but they don't necessarily involve reading aloud. For example: simply talking to the learners ('live listening'), and/or using video/DVD as a source for listening material.
Q3: Tasks that divert attention away from processing the text at the word level can help, e.g. matching, sequencing, selecting, etc. tasks. Learners' need to 'understand every word' can be satisfied towards the end of a task sequence, by giving them the transcript.

Q4: Songs can be used like any other listening text, but many do not lend themselves to in-depth scrutiny. The best are probably those that have some narrative element, and/or that include the repeated use of (useful) formulaic language. A diet solely of songs would probably not be a good idea, but their occasional use is likely to motivate many learners, especially if they are songs they have themselves chosen.

Q5: Coursebook texts may sound unnatural because – in order to control their level of difficulty, or to build into them specific language items – they have often been scripted and then recorded, rather than recorded spontaneously. Teachers can make their own unscripted, or semi-scripted, recordings, using colleagues or friends, but there is often a price to pay in terms of acoustic quality. Another source of more natural-sounding speech is authentic recorded material, such as TV and radio interviews, films, and soap operas.

Q6: One way of helping learners become 'strategic listeners' in interactive talk is to teach them some expressions with which they can control the input, such as *Do you mean …? Did you say …? I'm sorry, I didn't understand …*, etc. Practice interacting with each other, and with the teacher, obviously helps.

11 Developing reading skills

Main focus
To learn the basic principles of developing the reading skill, and to apply these to the design of a skills-based lesson.

Learning outcomes
- Trainees are aware of different purposes and strategies for reading.
- Trainees understand how comprehension is achieved in reading.

- Trainees apply these principles to the design of lessons aimed at developing reading skills.

Key concepts
- reading for information, gist, pleasure, intensive reading
- skimming, scanning
- top-down vs bottom-up knowledge
- linguistic vs extralinguistic clues
- pre-, while- and post-reading tasks

Stage	Focus
A Warm-up	introducing the topic through discussion questions
B Reading purposes and strategies	highlighting different reasons for, and ways of, reading texts
C Reading in a second language	experiencing reading in another language
D Coursebook reading texts and tasks	identifying the rationale behind coursebook reading tasks
E A reading lesson	ordering the stages of a reading lesson
Reflection	reviewing the issues discussed in this unit

A Warm-up

The following points could be made, in discussing these questions:

a Reading is like listening: both are receptive skills and involve the comprehension of text. The main difference is in the *mode* (written vs spoken language), and in the fact that listening takes place in *real time* whereas readers (usually) have time to read (and re-read) at their own pace.

b Vocabulary is important, but a knowledge of all the words does not guarantee comprehension, since other kinds of knowledge (such as grammar knowledge, and background knowledge of the topic) are also implicated.

c Reading aloud, on the part of the students, has only limited usefulness, can be very tedious, and may actually interfere with the successful understanding of a text. It is best avoided.

d Simplifying texts can make them more accessible to learners, but a diet of only simplified texts may not be the best preparation for 'real-life' reading.

e Reading is a good way of improving vocabulary, although more for receptive than for productive purposes. Moreover, classroom reading is seldom sufficient to trigger incidental vocabulary learning: it needs to be supplemented by a great deal of extra-class reading.

f Literary texts can provide variety as well as useful cultural knowledge, but most learners need to read for information rather than for pleasure.

g This is largely true, but the successful transfer of reading skills from one language to another depends on the reader having a core of language knowledge (e.g. vocabulary and grammar).

B Reading purposes and strategies

1 The completed chart should look like this: (Note that more than one way of reading may be possible, as the reader alternates between different modes, according to his or her purpose.)

Text type	Reason for reading		Way of reading		
	pleasure	information	close reading	skimming for gist	scanning for specific information
the instructions for installing a computer monitor		✓	✓		
a text message (SMS) from a friend		✓	✓	✓	
the evening's programmes in a TV guide		✓			✓
a newspaper report of a sports event		✓		✓	✓
a short story	✓		✓	✓	
a research paper published in a scholarly journal		✓	✓	✓	✓

Note the following points: Readers read some texts very closely (such as instructions) while other texts they may simply *skim*, in order to get the main *gist* (as, for example, in reading the report of a sports event, where they may be less interested in the detail than in the main facts). Readers may also *scan* a text, searching for a specific piece of information, as when they are consulting a TV guide. In actual fact, readers will probably apply several different strategies to the one text. Their purpose for reading the text – e.g. the need for specific information as opposed to getting the gist of a story – will determine the strategies they employ.

2 The main point to note here is that different text types will require different kinds of classroom tasks. For example, it would be inappropriate to ask learners to read an instruction manual just for gist, or to read a poem for specific information.

C Reading in a second language

1 Ask if anyone is familiar with Esperanto. If they are, ask them to imagine how an English speaker with no knowledge of Esperanto would process this text. Trainees should read the text individually and silently, and attempt to answer the questions.

2 Trainees can compare their answers to activity C1 in pairs.

   1 Even with limited knowledge of the language of the text, the reader can use a range of clues to 'decode' both the gist of it as well as identifying some specific facts. These clues include:

   - layout, type face, etc. which triggers background knowledge of this kind of text type (news report), including the way that news information is typically organised, i.e. main facts first, then background information;
   - the picture, which provides information about the topic;
   - words that are similar to English or other language words (e.g. *teatro, egipta, personoj*) as well as other *cross-linguistic* information, such as number and place names.

2 This suggests that learners do not need to know all the words in a text in order to be able to gain some understanding of its content. This in turn supports the case for using authentic (ungraded) texts with learners, even at relatively low levels.

3 Teachers can help learners understand texts by setting tasks that exploit their different kinds of knowledge. For example, the students can be asked to use their knowledge of text types and/or any *extralinguistic* information (such as pictures) and/or their background knowledge of the topic to make predictions as to the content of the text, in advance of reading it. They can also be asked to *skim* the text initially, using the words that they recognise, to give them a general idea of the gist, before a closer, more intensive reading.

D Coursebook reading texts and tasks

1 The purpose of these tasks can be summarised as:

a and b Using the picture to trigger background knowledge of the topic, and any related vocabulary that learners already know.

c Pre-teaching key vocabulary in order to make the text easier to understand (Tasks a, b and c are *pre-reading tasks*.)

d A general gist reading task, to give the students a purpose for reading, without encouraging them to read (and try to remember) every detail. (This is a *while-reading task*.)

e More detailed questions, to provide a purpose for a more detailed re-reading of the text. (This is probably another *while-reading task,* although the instruction to re-read the text is not explicit.)

f and g These tasks now focus attention on specific language features of the text, such as vocabulary. They are *post-reading tasks.*

h This is another post-reading task that requires learners to respond to the text in some way – in this case through writing.

2 a The features of the text that might help understanding include its *title* and the *illustration* (which allow the reader to predict the content of the text); topic familiarity, at least with other ball games, which helps make sense of potentially ambiguous words like *court, rings, pads;* and the logical organisation of the text into paragraphs, each with its own topic. Factors that might inhibit understanding include the use of rare or specialised vocabulary (*ritual, sacred, enactment; rectangular, sloping, diameter,* etc.), and the use of some 'higher level' grammar structures such as the passive (*was played, were divided,* etc.) and modal constructions (*would have weighed, must have made …*).

b Possible *pre-reading tasks* might include:

- using the picture and/or title to activate background knowledge and to brainstorm vocabulary (e.g. associated with ball games)
- pre-teaching unfamiliar vocabulary

Possible *while-reading tasks* might include:

- answering gist questions, e.g. how many players were there? what was the aim of the game? what was its significance? Or: how similar was this game to modern basketball?
- using the information to draw a ball court, or to choose the picture that best represents the game in action;
- answering more detailed questions, such as true/false, or multiple choice.

Post-reading tasks might include:

- focus on language features such as *modality*, by, for example, underlining all the *modal verbs* and other expressions of probability/possibility;
- write a description of modern day football or basket ball, from the point of view of a writer 1000 years from now.

E A reading lesson

1 The most logical order is probably: c, h, f, d, a, b, g, e.
2 For this task, it may be appropriate to use the coursebook that the trainees are using in their teaching practice. You may wish to assign particular sequences to look at. Encourage trainees to think of ways of extending the task sequence by, for example, adding stages that are mentioned in the previous task.

REFLECTION

These questions could be assigned to different groups, e.g., questions *a–d* to one group, questions *e–h* to another. The groups can then re-form and compare their responses, before a general, open-class discussion. Points that could be made here include:

a This extralinguistic information can help activate background knowledge, which in turn assists comprehension by compensating for lack of linguistic knowledge.
b Authentic materials may be more motivating for learners, even if challenging, and they are arguably better preparation for 'real-life' reading. They may also retain textual and extralinguistic features that assist comprehension, and that are lost in simplified or specially-written materials.
c A task provides the learners with a purpose for reading the text, and (depending on the choice of task) it can help divert the learners away from the temptation to focus on decoding the meaning of every word.
d If a text is of a type that is typically *scanned* (such as a TV guide), a task that 'matches' this text type would be a scanning one. On the other hand, if a text is of a type that is typically read intensively, such as a set of instructions, an appropriate task would be one which requires the students to process it in a similar, intensive, way. It is a good idea to match the tasks with the text, since such a matching is more likely to prompt learners to transfer their first language reading skills into their second language. Moreover it provides realistic preparation for real-life reading.
e In this way the focus is moved away from testing reading, to developing reading skills, i.e. *teaching* reading.
f Learners tend to over-rely on dictionaries unless trained in how to use them constructively. An alternative is to try to work out the meaning of unfamiliar words from context.
g The ability to recall the details of a text is a reliable gauge of understanding, but understanding is not dependent on memorising details. Most kinds of texts, in fact, are read for immediate understanding, not for later recall. Moreover, answering questions from memory is associated more with testing than with skills development.

12 Presenting language through texts

Main focus
To explore text-based ways of presenting grammar and vocabulary.

Learning outcomes
- Trainees review approaches to presenting new language items.
- Trainees understand how texts can be exploited to present grammar and vocabulary.
- Trainees can apply these understandings to the design of text-based presentation.

Key concepts
- context
- text (spoken and written)
- authenticity
- text-based teaching

Stage	Focus
A Warm-up	reviewing the stages of a grammar presentation
B Context	deciding on the features of a useful context for presentation
C Text-based presentations	identifying the stages of a text-based grammar presentation
D Classroom application	designing a text-based presentation
Reflection	reflecting on the pros and cons of text-based presentations

Note: This unit assumes familiarity with Unit 5 (on vocabulary presentation), Units 6 and 7 (on grammar presentation) and 10 and 11 (on receptive skills).

A Warm-up

1 This activity is designed to review aspects of grammar presentation covered in Units 6 and 7 Classroom Teaching. You may like to cut the sentence halves up and have trainees mingle to find their partner.
   Answers: 1–d); 2–c); 3–b); 4–a).
2 Other possible ways of presenting the meaning of the structure include:
   - a *real* situation, e.g. using the experience of one of the students, or the teacher's own experience
   - translation (only an option in mono-lingual groups)
   - paraphrase, explanation, e.g. we use this structure when we want to talk about something that began in the past and continues to the present
   - a context – which is the focus of this session.

B Context

1 Point out that 'context' is used in this unit to mean 'the surrounding text' (sometimes referred to as *co-text*) and that the surrounding text can be either spoken or written. For language presentation purposes, the same principles apply for both spoken and written texts, but, in the case of the former, it helps if there is a transcript that learners can study.

    1 Context a is an easily recognisable one and the sense of obligation is fairly clear; however, there is only one example of the target form, and the understanding of that is partly dependent on students understanding *babysit*. Context b, on the other hand, has several examples, and the sense of obligation is reinforced by synonymous expressions, such as *It's really important ... it's one of the rules*. Moreover, *have to* co-occurs with *don't have to*, which is clearly related to the meaning of *no obligation*. Context c has two examples of *have to*, but they both occur with *go*, and the context does not foreground the sense of obligation: *have to go* could equally well mean *want to go*, *(would) like to go*, or simply *go* or *am going* in these contexts. Context d has plenty of examples of *have to*, but so much so that it sounds unnatural, and there are few if any context clues to suggest that these activities are obligatory.

    2 Again, Context b displays the form well, since there are several examples; these occur with different personal pronouns, and there is an example in the negative. In Contexts a, c and d it would be difficult to infer these other forms.

2 A very general principle, which all the following points support, is that the context should provide enough data for the learners to work out the rules of meaning and form for themselves. Other principles might include:
- the context should be an easily recognisable and comprehensible one
- it should provide lots of clues as to the meaning of the target item
- it should help eliminate other, competing meanings
- there should be more than one example of the item, if possible (but not so many that the text sounds unnatural)
- the item should be displayed in a variety of forms

C Text-based presentations

1 The structure is the second conditional. The 'imaginative' use of this verb structure is clearly illustrated, not just in the text, but in the graphics. Moreover, the structure is repeated a number of times. There could be some problems, however, if learners didn't know some of the vocabulary, e.g. *budgie, palace, governess*, etc. Note that, at no point, is the learners' comprehension of the text checked.

2 The purpose of these stages are:
Stage 1 to check understanding of the concept;
Stage 2 to highlight the form;
Stage 3 to provide initial practice.

D Classroom application

1 Divide the class into pairs or small groups. Assign a text to each group. Tell the groups to plan a presentation based on their text, which they should be prepared to demonstrate, or at least 'talk through'. The presentation should include a stage where the learners' understanding of the text is facilitated, according to the principles and procedures outlined in Units 10 and 11. The language areas that they choose to highlight should be appropriate to the level, as indicated in the rubric.

a Language areas that might be exploited using these texts are:

Text a: language to talk about future plans, intentions, and wishes, e.g. *plan on + -ing, plan to + infinitive, will (+ probably/definitely)*, present continuous (*we're heading back*), *love to do, hope to do*. Also, positive appraisal language: (*sounds/it's been*) *great; favourite (place); love, enjoy; really friendly*; etc.

Text b: different types of transport; travel language (*travel, head (south), transport, journey, trek, arrive, complete*).

Text c: phrasal verbs, e.g. *work out, sort out, turn out*. Idioms and collocations: *beyond repair, take charge, a dressing down, strings attached, take [things] for granted*. Vocabulary of problems/solutions: *mistakes, stressful situation, tricky matter, issue, solution, resolved*; modal verbs for prediction: *might, could, will, going to*.

2 Representatives from each group can then demonstrate their 'lesson', using the other trainees as learners, or they can simply talk the rest of the class through their lesson plan. After each 'lesson', comment on the logic of the staging, and the appropriacy of choice of language focus.

REFLECTION

Points that could emerge from this discussion include:

a A text-based approach displays language 'at work', rather than in the form of de-contextualised sentences; it also allows learners to work rules out for themselves (assuming the texts are well chosen), which is good preparation for autonomous learning; it can also provide a natural follow-on to other text-based activities, such as skills development.

b Problems include: text difficulty, and the need to ensure comprehension of the text in advance of using it as a 'language object'; the artificiality of texts that are specially written to display numerous examples of a pre-selected item.

c Authentic texts have the advantage that the target items will (generally) be used in 'real life' ways, e.g. in association with other items that they naturally co-occur with. However, they may not occur with sufficient frequency for 'discovery learning' purposes. More problematic is the difficulty involved in processing the texts, which may preclude their use for language presentation purposes, except at higher levels.

13 Developing speaking skills

Main focus
Ways of developing speaking skills.

Learning outcomes
1 Trainees understand the main considerations in dealing with a speaking skills lesson.
2 Trainees understand the uses of a variety of speaking activities.

Key concepts
- communication, information gap
- task, discussion, roleplay, survey, presentation, game
- rehearsal, outcome, feedback

Stage	Focus
A Warm-up	trainees experience and reflect on a short speaking activity
B Different speaking activities	introducing a variety of speaking activities
C Challenges	introducing some practical considerations in dealing with speaking
D Questions and answers	introducing the role of the teacher in speaking lessons
Reflection	trainees put what they have learned into practice

A Warm-up

This section can be done without the trainees opening their books.

1 Set the activity up and then encourage trainees to reflect on their experience by answering the questions.
2 1 It assumes that learners can hold short conversations – so it would not be appropriate for very low level learners. However, a simple formula such as *Do you like…?* would enable learners to cope with it. It assumes that the learners will be comfortable sharing information about themselves.
   2 Speaking and listening – and potentially grammar points such as, *both of us, neither of us,* assuming that there is a stage in which learners report back on what they found out.
   3 To set up and manage the activity and to monitor learner output.
   4 Answers will vary but trainees need to justify their answer with reference to the issues in 1 and 2).
   5 The learners could be asked to report back on what they found out and the teacher could offer some feedback (correction and so on).

B Different speaking activities

1 If time allows, we suggest that the trainees do at least some of these activities. They could then reflect on the way the activities were set up and their potential for speaking practice. In this way you could, of course, replace any of the activities with others that you prefer. The trainees could work in small groups to discuss the questions and note down their responses in the grid. Encourage trainees to share their experience of using these types of activities, either in the TP lessons or in their previous experience.

If you are short of time, assign two or three activities to each group of trainees, rather than have them consider all the activities.

The following summarises the main points that should emerge from this task:

a Is it practical?

   1 Discussion: Easy to set up; less easy to monitor; helps if learners are given planning time.

   2 Roleplay: Learners need to understand their role and this may sometimes involve lengthy reading. They are asked to voice opinions that may not be their own and this may demand preparation time as they think of arguments, etc.

   3 Survey/presentation: Some preparation will be required before the survey, as learners formulate questions. Also they will need to prepare before reporting back their findings.

   4 Guessing game: Generally fairly little preparation but – see d). Some games can have quite complex instructions, but it will depend on the exact activity being used.

   5 Information gap: Yes, they are generally easy to set up and quickly understood by learners.

b Is it purposeful?

   1 Discussion: No real outcome to this task, but might be made more purposeful if learners had to persuade each other and reach a consensus and/or report the discussion to the class.

   2 Roleplay: This may depend on the roleplay, but usually there is a purpose: in this case it's a resolution to a problem.

   3 Survey/presentation: There is an outcome from the survey (the report). But the reporting back may not engage those that are not actually speaking.

   4 Guessing game: Yes – solving the problem or 'winning' the game.

   5 Information gap: Typically it is purposeful because learners share information to solve a problem or complete a task of some kind, as in this case.

c Is it productive?

   1 Discussion: If learners are not engaged with the topic, discussions can fall flat; can be rather academic; helps if there is a purpose (see (b)).

   2 Roleplay: Some learners may resent the artificiality of the roleplay – topics need to be chosen that the learners can relate to and are interested in.

   3 Survey/presentation: Yes, if learners are asked to give a presentation they will produce a fair amount of language in most cases.

   4 Guessing game: This will vary with the type of game.

   5 Information gap: Yes – learners must participate in order to complete the task.

d Is it predictable?

   1 Discussion: Some vocabulary is predictable and learners are also likely to practise agreeing/disagreeing, interrupting and so on. However, the majority of language use is unpredictable.

2 Roleplay: This will depend on the roleplay, but a roleplay of a service encounter, for example, is usually highly predictable.

3 Survey/presentation: Yes – this will be determined by the topic of the survey/ presentation. Learners can prepare survey questions in advance, and can prepare and rehearse presentations, making the language used in both cases highly predictable.

4 Guessing game: Fairly predictable, meaning that lower level learners can be prepared for the activity if necessary.

5 Information gap: Usually very predictable as the design of the task can be manipulated to elicit particular language. The example given here would be good for the present continuous for future arrangements.

e **Is it adaptable?**

1 Discussion: Assumes a fairly advanced level; easier topics could be chosen for lower levels.

2 Roleplay: Very adaptable. Roleplays can be used with almost any level, although at lower levels they are likely to be short. Learners can experiment with language in different contexts and practise a variety of styles/registers.

3 Survey/presentation: Yes, topics and specific tasks can be designed that will appeal to a range of learners.

4 Guessing game: Activities such as these are often used with lower levels, but an example such as the one given would work with a higher level class.

5 Information gap: Very adaptable and are frequently used in communicative language teaching, particularly as they can be designed to elicit the use of particular language items.

2 Ask the trainees to choose one of the above activities or assign them one. They can work in pairs to decide how they will set up the activity and to prepare instructions for it. You could then nominate two or three trainees to give their instructions and ask the group to comment on their appropriacy and clarity.

C Challenges

1 The second part of this section is a summary of the points raised in the first part. Allow the trainees some time to discuss the comments by learners before reporting back their ideas and then completing the table. If you are short of time, you might like to assign just one or two of the learner comments to each pair or group of trainees.

	What I can learn from the learner
Cinzia	Learners can feel very intimidated if the teacher demands that they speak. Ideally the classroom should be a safe and relaxing place in which learners can experiment and practise with language. Teachers need to try to create a relaxed environment. At lower levels, learners may need quite a lot of preparation before they are ready to undertake a speaking task.
Hyun-Joo	Teachers need to consider the cultural differences that exist between themselves and learners. Topics that the teacher may feel comfortable discussing may not be considered appropriate by everybody.
Danijela	Different learners will have different tastes – and so teachers need to include a variety of activity types in order to appeal to as many people as possible.

	What I can learn from the learner
Alejandra	Speaking is extremely difficult if you don't know what to say. Teachers need to ensure that learners are thoroughly prepared for activities – in this case, for example, brainstorming ideas would have helped.
Ali	Speaking is more than knowing words and how to combine them. There are some socio-cultural skills to learn too. How long is it appropriate to speak for? How can you interrupt? How is your turn 'signalled'? etc.
Anja	Particularly at higher levels, it can be hard for learners to see the point of speaking activities. The teacher needs to consider how the value can be demonstrated – for example by giving plenty of feedback to learners both on what was good and how their performance could be improved.
Vera	While not all learners may want to speak, it is very important that the teacher ensures that those that do want to speak get opportunities to do so. Sometimes the teacher can help by forming groups based on level – so that all the stronger learners are together and also the weaker ones are together – this will reduce the risk of weaker learners being dominated by stronger peers.

D Questions and answers

1 The activity is designed to reinforce some of the points covered and also to deal briefly with some practical considerations in setting up and dealing with speaking lessons.
The answers to the activity are: 1–c) 2–d) 3–b) 4–f) 5–a) 6–e)

2 Invite and answer any similar questions that the trainees may have.

REFLECTION

This activity can be done without trainees referring to the instructions in the trainee book. Allow the trainees time to prepare. You may like to structure the feedback in a pyramid fashion – with pairs joining to make fours, and then eights and so on, before concluding with an open class discussion.

14 Developing writing skills

Main focus

Ways of developing writing skills.

Learning outcomes

1 Trainees understand the principle of writing as a process.
2 Trainees understand ways of developing writing skills in a classroom context.
3 Trainees understand the rationale behind ways of responding to written work.

Key concepts

- communication, readership
- text-type
- product vs process writing
- model text; drafts
- correcting writing, responding to writing

Stage	Focus
A Warm-up	introducing some practical considerations and background issues in teaching writing
B Writing activities	introducing some writing activities
C Stages in writing	introducing the idea of writing as a process
D Marking written work	introducing ways of responding to writing
E Classroom application	trainees identify stages in a writing lesson and then implement them in their own design of a lesson
Reflection	trainees reflect on what they have learned by doing a short writing task

There is one optional activity that supports the unit. It involves responding to learner writing.

A Warm-up

You could elicit the views of some of the trainees before starting this activity. They could talk about their experiences of dealing with writing in TP, or of learning to write in other languages.

1 Allow the trainees to work in small groups to discuss their ideas before reporting back. You may wish to highlight some of the following points:
   a Tracy: It is a common view that writing can be done almost exclusively outside the class. However, some stages of a writing lesson that can be done usefully in class – thinking of ideas, discussing and organising ideas, group writing, working on editing skills, etc.
   b Korali: Learners always need lots of varied practice of grammar and vocabulary and the fact that they are under less time pressure when they write means that writing is a useful mode for a focus on accuracy. However, to use this mode exclusively for language practice ignores the fact that writing is a skill in its own right, and one that (arguably) needs to be developed through practice.

c David: It is probably right to pick out only some of the errors. If a learner gets a piece of work back which is covered in corrections it can be demotivating. It is also a good idea to respond, not just to the form of the message (including its errors) but also to its content, as this reinforces the idea that writing is a means of communication, not just a way of practising grammar and spelling.

d Paula: It is probably right to think of ways that writing activities can be made fun and not be intimidating to learners. On the other hand, simply doing writing for self-expression ignores the fact that many learners (e.g. those who need English for academic or professional purposes) need to master text types where a high premium is placed on accuracy.

e Hassan: This point of view is reasonable, but overlooks the fact that the weaker learners may be getting support from the stronger ones, and hence learning from them.

B Writing activities

1 You may prefer to demonstrate one activity, for example the text messaging (c). Afterwards analyse the activity, drawing attention to the sorts of issues raised in the table. The trainees could then discuss another activity that contrasts with the first (for example, d).

Ensure that the trainees understand the criteria for categorising the different tasks. It may help to complete one of the rows in open class. Then, allow the trainees to work in pairs to discuss their answers before they report back.

Note that a writing task is 'communicative' if it requires writers to communicate meanings in order to affect the thoughts or behaviours of their reader(s). The production of sentences or texts in order to practise specific grammatical or textual features, although perfectly justifiable as a form of practice, is unlikely to be communicative. A text is 'integrated' if it forms a complete 'message' in a recognisable text type, even if it is part of a series of messages (as in the case of text-messaging). As for authenticity, a task can be 'real-life-like' even if it's not something that the learners themselves expect to do in real life, e.g. write a poem.

You may want to point out that none of the activities is inherently 'better' or 'worse' than any of the others, but that those where there is a high number of 'no' answers probably do not in themselves provide sufficient preparation for the skill of writing.

Analysis of activity types					
Activity type	Communicative purpose	Integration	Authenticity	Readership	Level
a Gap fill	no	no	no	no	all levels
b Reproducing model	no (unless stipulated in the task rubric)	yes	yes (if the model text is real-life-like)	no (unless stipulated in the task rubric)	most levels (depending on model text)
c Interactive writing	yes	yes	yes	yes	all levels
d Composition	no (unless stipulated)	yes	no	no (unless stipulated)	intermediate and upwards
e Dialogue + items	no	yes	no	no	most levels

2 Trainees can discuss the activity in pairs or small groups, before reporting back. One way of re-designing the activity to make it more communicative, more integrated, more authentic, and of providing a readership, might be:

> **Your favourite pop group is coming to your town shortly. Write an email to a friend, who doesn't know about this group, and try to persuade the friend to come to see them with you, giving lots of reasons.**

C Stages in writing

1 Allow trainees to work individually for a minute or two before comparing with each other in pairs and then agreeing an appropriate order with you. You could point out that these stages may overlap to some extent. A logical order might be: d, c, b, a, e.

2 Proponents of a 'process approach' to writing would argue that writing in the classroom needs to be treated as a staged process, with attention being given to each stage. Examples are given in 3, below.

3 You may prefer to choose a writing task from a coursebook that the trainees are currently using, but the task should embody at least some features of a process approach.
Part a – the learners read the email and identify the information requested. This helps them to understand the model text and gives ideas for what could be included during the writing phase.
Part b – the learners analyse some of the language used in the email. In this case they consider the formal expressions and try to think of more informal equivalents. This phase focuses on some of the language that the learners will need for the task.
Part c – the learners choose a course and write an email requesting information. By having more than one course advert, there is a better chance that the learners will be able to write about something they are interested in. This is in effect a first draft. Notice the instruction that follows (check your email for grammar, spelling and punctuation) which encourages an editing stage.

4 Trainees may have various ideas about how the material could be adapted. For example, they may suggest having a phase of discussing ideas at the start. They may suggest that the writing be done in pairs or small groups, or that the adverts are substituted for genuine ones whereby the learners can write real emails and (perhaps) get a reply.

D Marking written work

As an alternative to the procedure here, you could collect some samples of writing from learners in TP classes and photocopy them for trainees to correct.

You may like to lead into this activity by asking trainees about their recollections of how teachers marked their work at school, particularly anything written in a foreign language.

1 Ask them to look at the three samples of types of marking and allow them to discuss their ideas in pairs briefly. If you need to, prompt the trainees to think about which method(s) involve the learners and also ask them to consider how much guidance the learners get. The final method (using the code) both involves learners and gives guidance and is very much part of a 'process view' of writing. On the downside, it can be very time consuming for both

teachers and learners – not least, because the teacher needs to check that corrections have been made appropriately.

2 At very low levels it may be hard for the learners to make the corrections themselves.

3 The key to the code is below, but you may wish to stress to the trainees that this is only an example – they could alter it to suit themselves and their learners. It is also worth pointing out that classifying errors is exceptionally complicated and there is some overlap here. All 'tense' errors are also 'grammar' errors, for example.

ww = wrong word   T = tense
sp = spelling   P = punctuation
wo = word order   un = unnecessary word
G = grammar   + = add a word, or part of a word

You may want to use the optional activity at this point.

E Classroom application

Organise the class into small groups and assign a task to each group. They can then report back in open class on the results of their discussion. At this stage, highlight features of their 'lesson plans' that conform to either a model-driven approach, or a process approach, to the teaching of writing. Emphasise the need to make writing tasks communicative, real-life-like, and reader-focused.

REFLECTION

1 Allow the trainees a little time to write their sentences before comparing them with a partner and then sharing some with the class. The aim is to review the key parts of this unit. If trainees do not include the following ideas, you can feed them in as you see fit.
Writing is both a way of communicating and is also used in the classroom as a learning aid and a way of practising language. Writing can be done collaboratively and tasks often work best when it is clear who will read the piece of writing – either another member of the class or a fictitious recipient. You might like to point out that different genres have different characteristics (some of which can be taught fairly easily).

2 You might like to ask the trainees to reflect on the activity and whether they enjoyed it, whether they felt they had had enough preparation and so on.

Optional activity

Photocopy a short piece of a learner's writing (about 100 words) and ask the trainees to correct it in the way which seems most appropriate to them.

15 Integrating skills

Main focus
A review of procedures aimed at developing skills and seeing how they can be combined within a single lesson.

Learning outcomes
1 Trainees understand the main considerations in dealing with integrated skills lessons.
2 Trainees are able to analyse integrated skills activities.
3 Trainees understand how language learning can be integrated into content teaching.

Key concepts
- receptive vs productive skills
- content-based learning
- authentic materials

Stage	Focus
A Warm-up	trainees experience and reflect on a short integrated skills activity
B Combining skills	trainees consider how the same skill may be treated differently in different contexts
C Classroom application	trainees analyse a piece of material
D Integrating content and language	studying a content-based teaching sequence
Reflection	trainees play a short game which reviews skills work

A Warm-up

This activity can be set up without the trainees opening their books.

1 You need one copy of the text below for each pair of trainees. Stick the copies around the room. One person in each pair should run to the text, read a chunk, go back to their partner and dictate it. The listener should write down what they hear and the 'runner' should go back for the next part. The winners are the first pair to finish. As pairs finish, take a copy of the text off the wall and ask them to compare what they have written with the original. Pairs who finish early can consider the question at the end of the text.

> You get a text message, you read it and you text back. You read an interesting newspaper story and you tell someone about it. You go to a lecture and you take notes. And you pass on some juicy gossip that you just heard. So, outside the classroom, language skills are not always used in isolation. They tend to be combined. Think back to the last lesson you taught. Were any skills combined?

2 Allow the trainees a little time to gather their ideas before reporting back in open class.

   1 The reader will predominantly practise reading and speaking. The writer will predominantly practise writing and listening.

   2 Usually the physical movement and competitive nature of the activity make it quite energising.

   3 This particular text may not be appropriate, but the activity would work in a variety of different contexts. Point out to trainees that language skills are not always used in isolation outside the classroom, for example, when we read a newspaper story that we find interesting we often tell someone about it. At a presentation or lecture that is important we might take notes. We read a text message and text back. A conversation involves speaking and listening.

B Combining skills

1 The trainees could do this activity in small groups.

Activity	listening	speaking	reading	writing
a Learners do a 15-minute role play in pairs. Half the class are journalists, who interview the other half of the class, who are famous actors.	✓	✓		
b Learners work briefly in small groups to discuss ideas to put into a piece of writing on animal rights. They then write a magazine-style article on the subject.	✓	✓		✓
c Learners read a text about language teaching methodologies and answer questions. They discuss their answers in small groups before reporting back to the teacher.	✓	✓	✓	
d Learners read a short newspaper description of a radio programme. They then listen to the radio programme and answer questions.	✓		✓	
e Learners work in pairs to write a review of a restaurant they like.	✓	✓		✓
f Learners make notes as they listen to a short recorded lecture.	✓			✓

2 1 The aim of this section is to demonstrate to trainees that a particular skill will not always have the same degree of prominence in all lessons. This will have implications for teaching. One or two examples should suffice to make the point, but you may wish to add others.

   2 Examples: a teacher may want to correct errors when speaking is the main focus, but when learners are speaking to compare answers to a listening comprehension exercise the teacher may choose to ignore all errors other than those that affect understanding. If reading is the main focus of an activity then the teacher may wish to set several reading tasks on the same text and, indeed, to select a text that will challenge learners. But if

reading is used as a way of contextualising a grammar point, then the teacher may prefer to choose a text which is relatively easy to understand and set only a single comprehension exercise, so that the lesson can move forwards to the grammar.

3 Explain the activity to the trainees. Allow them to work together before reporting back in open class. An alternative focus for this activity could be the trainees' own lessons in TP: ask them to reflect on a lesson they have taught recently, and to identify the different skills it involved. Were there opportunities for yet more integration? This activity would work best if trainees were organised into their TP groups.

C Classroom application

There are various ways the text could be exploited and you may like to give an example or two at the start so that trainees are clear on what is expected of them. It could be read aloud to the class as if it were a news item, or dictated, or in the form of a dictogloss (listening); the learners could read it themselves (reading); they could discuss it, saying whether they think the prediction is likely or not, and what the implications might be (speaking and listening); they could brainstorm the questions that the aliens would ask (speaking and writing); they could interview Dr Seth Shostak in the form of a roleplay (speaking and listening); they could write the news story describing the first communications from outer space (writing); they could role play the first communication between aliens and humans (speaking and listening), or do this in the form of emails or text messages (writing and reading).

Note: You may wish to choose a text that is more topical, or one that is more relevant to the trainees' own classes.

D Integrating content and language

1 There is a focus on grammar in stages d–f.
   a speaking and listening (to each other)
   b reading
   c speaking and listening (to each other)
   g listening (to a recording)
   h writing (and possibly reading each other's texts)

2 Trainees may make the following points:
   1 The material is similar to a standard coursebook sequence in that it combines varied skills work with a focus on grammar; it is different only in that the topic is one associated with subject teaching rather than language teaching.
   2 The main advantage is that learners are learning both the language and the content simultaneously, which makes this approach particularly appropriate for younger learners. A disadvantage is that insufficient language knowledge may inhibit the learning of the content. The teacher needs to ensure that the material is intelligible, e.g. by checking comprehension, using simplified texts, and taking 'time off' to deal with language issues.
   3 A content-based approach should work equally well for adults, although the nature of the content will depend on the learners' needs and interests. This issue will be revisited in Unit 22: English for Special Purposes.

REFLECTION

Explain how to play the game. You may have to act as a 'referee' if there is a disputed answer. Summarise the answers after the groups have finished.

1 Reading and listening
2 Writing and speaking
3 A text that has not been produced with language teaching as its purpose. Examples of authentic texts will vary, but newspapers, magazines and so on are typical examples.
4 Because they can use context clues and background knowledge to 'fill in the gaps'. Or, in some cases, parts of the text may not be relevant to them.
5 Various answers are possible – the recording could be periodically stopped, the tapescript given out, more vocabulary could be pre-taught, and so on.
6 Trainees could talk about things such as brainstorming ideas, collaborating on a first draft, editing the first draft (by finding errors and so on) and producing a final draft, perhaps for homework.
7 Whenever learners speak, it is usually the case that someone will be listening.
8 Various answers are possible, but some suggestions would be that trainees could read a model answer or read input data (such as a letter that they have to respond to). They could discuss the content of what to write (speaking/listening) and so on.
9 Combining listening and writing is difficult at low levels. The concentration on producing the writing can leave little brain space for focusing on the text and understanding it.
10 Again, there are many possibilities, which include: writing a letter or email of complaint, and discussing their own holiday experiences.
11 The text should be interesting to the learners. The text should also be of an appropriate length and complexity.

16 Lesson planning: design and staging

> **Main focus**
> Designing and staging lessons.
>
> **Learning outcomes**
> 1 Trainees understand the principles of planning a balanced lesson.
> 2 Trainees can apply these principles in order to structure a plan for a lesson on language systems.
>
> **Key concepts**
> - staging, sequencing
> - pace, variety
> - interaction pattern
> - lesson aims, anticipated problems, class profile, procedure

Stage	Focus
A Warm-up	introducing the topic of planning
B Sequencing stages	trainees consider options for staging a systems lesson
C Planning decisions	trainees consider interaction patterns and variety
D Putting it on paper	trainees consider the requirements of formal lesson plans
E Procedures	trainees recreate a lesson plan
Reflection	trainees reflect on what they have learned

> Defining lesson aims is dealt with in Unit 17.
> Alternative approaches to lesson design are dealt with in Unit 18.
> Planning a scheme of work is dealt with in Unit 19.

A Warm-up

1 and 2 Allow the trainees some time to finish their chosen sentences. If you have time, allow them to mingle to find a partner who completed the same sentence and to compare their endings. Get them to report back in open class. The following are suggestions:

   a a film – has a structure of beginning, middle and end. The beginning has to create interest and the end give a sense of closure. Parts may be predictable, but other parts may provide twists and surprises.

   b a football match – has pace (although this will vary at different stages of the match) and energy. Trainees may compare the roles of teachers and coaches, or teachers and referees.

   c a meal – (in three courses) again has a beginning, middle and end structure and closure at the end. A meal is a combination of ingredients that complement each other.

   d a symphony – has a predictable structure, a variety of pace and a theme or themes that run through it

3 You may like to do this in open class, considering just one metaphor, if you think that your trainees will find this very difficult. You may expect some kind of introduction that would

also serve to contextualise the language. There will be a presentation phase of some kind, where the meaning and form are conveyed and checked. There will be plenty of varied practice activities. There will be a sense of completion at the end of the lesson.

B Sequencing stages

You may prefer to use a plan for a lesson that the trainees have seen. This could come from an observation task, for example.

1 Allow the trainees to work in pairs or small groups before comparing their ideas with each other and you. A suggested answer is below. Point out that task checking stages are not included in this plan. You may like to ask trainees at what points they would expect there to be some task checking. (e.g. after Stages 2, 3, 5)

2 Having established the order of the stages, you could ask the trainees to provide a very brief rationale for each.

Stage	Time	Procedure
1	0–5	c The teacher asks learners about their favourite stories when they were young. Learners volunteer stories.
2	6–10	f The teacher gives out a short story and asks learners to underline examples of the past simple in blue and underline examples of the past continuous in red.
3	11–18	d The teacher clarifies the form with examples on the board and then gives out a series of rules of use of the verb forms. Learners decide which rules go with which verb form and pick out examples from the text.
4	19–20	b The teacher asks questions to check understanding.
5	21–28	e Learners complete sentences, deciding whether the past simple or continuous is more appropriate.
6	29–35	a The teacher divides the class into three groups. Each group makes up a story.
7	36–45	g The teacher forms new groups, comprising one person from each of the other groups. The learners tell each other their stories.

C Planning decisions

1 Check that trainees understand the abbreviations used in the interaction pattern descriptions. Confirm their answers.

Activity	Procedure	Interaction
Speaking	The learners talk about their hobbies and interests in groups	Ss–Ss
Task checking/ report back	The teacher asks the learners what they talked about	Ss–T
Reading for gist	The learners read a text quickly to understand the gist of it (questions 1–3 on handout)	Ss–text
Checking answers	Learners compare answers to reading	Ss–Ss

2 Allow the trainees some time to look at the exercise and think of ways in which it could be extended. One way would be for learners to do a mingle activity in which they try to find people with whom they have things in common.

D Putting it on paper

You may like to use this as an opportunity to reinforce the requirements of planning at your centre and the pro forma plans that are in use.

1 1–c) 2–d) 3–b) 4–e) 5–a)

2 and 3 This section encourages trainees to anticipate difficulties in three areas – linguistic, organisational, and those based on individual learner needs.

  a organisational – the teacher could use one group of three.

  b individual – the teacher could nominate other learners to answer.

  c organisational/individual – the teacher could try to integrate students more in a multi-lingual class (i.e. mix nationalities up) or, with a monolingual group could avoid putting these particular learners together, introduce rules about when the L1 can be used. Not letting activities go on too long, giving clear instructions are also useful ways of limiting the opportunities to use L1.

  d individual – the teacher could nominate the learner and use structured pairwork where she is not put on the spot, but has to contribute.

  e linguistic – the teacher could do some practice with word stress, e.g. choral drilling of the target structures before a freer activity.

E Procedures

You will need one copy of the plan on page 75 for each group. Cut up the plan so that all the boxes are separate (there will be 21 pieces in all). Write the headings *Stage/Time, Procedure, Aim* on the board. Put the trainees into groups of two or three, and ask them to piece the plan back together, using the three headings to organise the pieces.

As groups finish, you may like them to move around the room and either help other groups, or simply observe other groups and compare answers. Your feedback could be done via copying the plan above for each member of the class. As an extra follow-up, you could ask them to describe the interaction pattern of each stage of the above lesson.

REFLECTION

Divide the trainees into small groups and ask them to discuss some of the statements that interest them. You may like to prompt, by asking things, e.g.: 'Which teacher do you identify with most?' 'What are some of the advantages and disadvantages of the approaches described?' etc.

Karina: What she says is true, but it should be balanced against the fact that no coursebook writer knows the particular class that is being taught and the teacher needs to tailor the material to the needs of the learners. In addition there are benefits to varying the style of lessons from time to time.

Kaylea: Many trainees may identify with what she says. However, after the course they may have to teach 25 or 30 lessons a week and so may have to modify their planning. Too much time spent on planning may leave no time for other forms of professional development.

Tom: This is probably close to the experience of many people – and the message may be reassuring for some trainees!

Maria: Again, this may be something that more experienced teachers feel confident enough to do. One way of encouraging trainees to adopt such an approach is to include some shorter TP sessions (e.g. about 20 minutes) as these will be less daunting. Provide them with a short speaking activity (5–10 minutes) and then ask them to work with the language produced for a further 10 minutes or so (for example, through a feedback/correction phase).

Richard: Trainees need to realise that lesson plans are not 'written in stone' and there will be times that adapting or even abandoning the plan are necessary. You could remind trainees that they need to keep in mind what they are trying to achieve in the lesson, so that they can make such decisions in as principled a way as possible.

Stage/Time	Procedure	Aim
Introduction 0–05	Teacher tells a short anecdote about finding a wallet in the street, and invites the learners to ask questions, e.g. 'What did you do?' 'Was there money in it?'	To introduce the theme of the lesson.
Spoken interaction 06–10	The teacher asks: 'What would you do if you found a wallet/$100/a mobile phone, etc. on the street?' Learners discuss their responses in pairs. Teacher asks individuals to report back.	To create a need for the new structure. To diagnose the extent of learners' existing knowledge.
Focus on target language item 11–15	Teacher elicits a model sentence – if necessary by saying, 'Can you give me a sentence beginning with 'If'?' Teacher models the sentence and learners repeat it.	To involve learners and to give them the opportunity to produce the target item. To highlight the spoken form.
Rule focus 16–20	Teacher writes model sentence on the board, and asks questions about it. For example: 'Is this sentence about the past?' 'What is 'd short for?'	To check that learners understand the concept and form of the new item.
Practice 1 21–30	Learners complete a gap fill of 2nd conditional sentences. Teacher monitors. Learners compare answers. Teacher checks task.	To provide initial accuracy practice.
Practice 2 31–50	Learners work in groups to devise a questionnaire, using the sentence stem, 'What would you do if ...' They then re-group and ask their questions to one another. They report their answers to the class.	To provide communicative and personalised practice of the new item
Feedback 51–55	Teacher highlights good examples of language use noticed in the lesson and some errors.	To encourage learners. To help them learn from their errors.

© Cambridge University Press 2007

17 Lesson planning: defining aims

Main focus

Trainees learn to distinguish and describe different kinds of lesson aims.

Learning outcomes

1 Trainees understand the differences between types of aims.
2 Trainees are able to analyse material and identify appropriate aims.
3 Trainees can apply their understanding, allowing them to write appropriate lesson and stage aims.

Key concepts

• linguistic aims, communicative aims, skills aims and interpersonal aims
• main aims, subsidiary aims

Stage	Focus
A Warm-up	trainees consider the importance and purpose of defining lesson aims
B Types of aims	trainees compare different types of lesson aim
C Material and aims	trainees identify the aims of pieces of material and practise wording accompanying aims
Reflection	trainees reflect on what they have learned

There are two optional activities which support the unit.

Optional activity 1 – Trainees identify how a piece of authentic material could be exploited.

Optional activity 2 – Trainees review the aims of the upcoming teaching practice lessons.

A Warm-up

Check that the trainees understand the terms used. Give them a few moments to tick the ones that they agree with and then they should mingle to find a partner who has ticked the same, or very similar, statements. The trainees then work with their new partner to agree their order of importance, before reporting back their ideas.

a … *trainers (and directors of studies) require them.* While this is true, it is not an end in itself and it is important that trainees do not see defining aims as solely an imposition.

b … *they make planning easier.* This is a strong argument for defining an aim for a lesson. If teachers know what they are trying to achieve it should be easier to select material and so on. It should also be easier to make decisions during the lesson in a principled way (which activities to extend, which to leave out, for example). However, there are also many other factors that become apparent during a lesson that influence such decisions – previous knowledge, levels of interest, and so on.

c … *they make lesson plans look more professional.* It is the content of the aims that is important, rather than the inclusion of any aim, regardless of what it says.

d ... *they frame the criteria by which the lesson will be judged.* This is relevant to the immediate course, where trainees will be asked to justify their lesson planning decisions; in their future practice having a clearly defined lesson aim will make self-evaluation easier.

e ... *learners need to know the focus of the lesson.* This may be true for many learners, although it is no guarantee of course that they will successfully learn.

f ... *they set a goal that can be used to test the learners' achievement.* This is a valid reason, especially when aims are framed in the form: *By the end of the lesson, learners will be able to ...*

B Types of aims

1 Trainees can work in pairs or small groups. The point of this task is to show that one lesson can share a number of interrelated aims, depending on the viewpoint that is taken. In this particular case, all the aims, apart from (c) (expressing future plans ...) seem compatible, since it's easy to imagine a lesson that focuses on the present perfect *and* talking about experience *and* informal conversation, etc.

2 communicative aim = b, c
interpersonal aim = f
linguistic aim = a
skills aim = d
developmental aim = e

3 This activity can be used to introduce the concept of a *main aim*, e.g. (e) and a *subsidiary* or *secondary aim*, e.g. (b). The wording that best matches the teacher's lesson description is (e). The problems of the other wordings are:

a too vague
b this doesn't appear to be the main aim
c too general, and not the main aim
d this is a potted description of what will happen, but is not an aim as such
f too vague, and not the main aim

4 a Lesson A: The main aim is the contrast of the verb forms. In the process of achieving this, the learners are going to do some reading practice.
Lesson B: The main aim is to develop speaking skills; the subsidiary aim is to introduce and practise some evaluative language.

b Lesson A: By the end of the lesson, the learners will have understood the difference between the present perfect simple and continuous. They will also have read and understood a short text.
Lesson B: By the end of the lesson, the learners will be able to talk about recent activities. To do this they will also be able to use some evaluative language.

C Material and aims

1 a *Intermediate Matters*
Main aim: to practise regular and irregular past simple forms (linguistic aim)
Possible subsidiary aim: to practise intensive reading skills (based on a newspaper article) (skills-focused aim)

b *Innovations pre-intermediate*
Main aim: oral fluency – to practise talking about situations in the past where something has gone wrong (communicative aim)
Possible subsidiary aim: to practise using past forms in spoken language (linguistic aim)

c *Grammar Games*
Main aim: to identify errors in the use of the present perfect with *for* and *since* (linguistic aim)
Possible subsidiary aim: to develop oral fluency in the context of playing and managing a game (skills-focused aim)

2 There may be variations in how these are expressed but should obviously relate closely to activity C1. You may want to reinforce any particular phraseology used at your centre.

REFLECTION

The trainees should report back in open class, having discussed the questions in groups. You may like to highlight:

Andrew: This is hard to answer definitively and you may like to prompt trainees to think of what other information they might need. One obvious point may be the level of the class – was it a challenge for the learners to speak in English? What did the teacher do with the language produced – was there any feedback? The probability is that the lesson was supposed to practise reading and the teacher should have ensured there was time for it.

Sophie: Variety of pace can be important. There is no reason why some of the controlled practice could not have been done after the game when perhaps, having made mistakes, the learners would more easily perceive the need for it.

Sam: Trainees need to be careful not to include too much new language in a single presentation phase.

Optional activity 1

It is possible to exploit the same piece of material in different ways to achieve different aims.

Work in groups.
Group A: Read the text and plan a lesson exploiting the material to practise both receptive and productive skills.
Group B: Read the text and plan a lesson using the material to introduce and/or practise a grammar pattern.

To Tip or Not to Tip: There Should Be a Hot Line

My tipping life did not start out well. I was fifteen and had just moved to New York to study dancing. (I know this is shocking to parents of fifteen-year-olds, but this is pretty common among headstrong kids who want to be dancers.) Anyway, I finished my first turkey sandwich in a coffee shop all by myself and picked up my dance bag and strolled out of the restaurant with my feet pointing outward so everyone would know I was a dancer. I didn't get half a block when I heard footsteps running up behind me. I'd only been in New York one day. Was I being mugged already? And aren't they supposed to be quieter than that? The mugger tapped me on the shoulder. I turned around. It was my waiter, and he was angry.

'You forgot to leave me a tip,' he said.
'A what?' I said.
'A tip. I served you a turkey sandwich and you gave me nothing.'
I panicked and took out my wallet and gave it to him. 'Take what you want, just don't hurt me.' He took out five dollars and handed me back my wallet.
'That's one dollar for serving you the turkey sandwich and four dollars for making me run down the street.'
'Why don't you take two dollars for serving me the sandwich and three dollars for running down the street?' I said, still not fully understanding the concept.

Naked Beneath My Clothes Rita Rudner

© Cambridge University Press 2007

Trainer's notes for optional activity 1

A: The text could be exploited to develop reading comprehension skills. It could also be used as a springboard for a discussion of tipping and differences between cultures. It could also be used to develop writing skills (for example, write the story from the perspective of the waiter).

B: The text could be used to present narrative forms (past simple, past progressive and past perfect all occur). The text could also be used to practise reported speech (by reporting the direct speech towards the end of this extract). In addition, like most texts, this could be exploited to highlight the use of high frequency items, such as articles. The extract could also be used to highlight cohesion and coherence and the other features that make it a text (rather than a collection of random sentences).

Optional activity 2

Review the aims of your next teaching practice session. Consider any rewording that is necessary. Then explain any changes you have made and your reasons for making them to a partner.

18 Alternative approaches to lesson design

Main focus
Approaches that foreground fluency and personalisation.

Learning outcomes
1 Trainees understand how to foreground fluency and personalisation of language.
2 Trainees have a basic understanding of task-based learning.
3 Trainees understand the rationale behind activities and lesson sequences based on approaches that foreground the learners' meanings.

Key concepts
- fluency-first
- test–teach–test; task-based learning
- Community Language Learning (CLL)
- personalisation

Stage	Focus
A Warm-up	considering the relationship between accuracy and fluency
B Two lesson designs	comparing two lesson formats and considering the effects of foregrounding fluency
C Task-based learning	examining the task cycle and how to exploit tasks
D Other lesson formats	activities based on learner-generated language
Reflection	trainees consider how they can apply what they have learned

There is one optional activity that supports the unit, in which trainees adapt coursebook material to allow for an approach that prioritises communication and fluency.

A Warm-up

1 Trainees can complete the text individually, and then compare answers with a partner. The answers are: (1) accuracy; (2) fluency; (3) fluency; (4) accuracy; (5) accuracy; (6) fluency; (7) fluency; (8) accuracy; (9) fluency.
2 Allow trainees to respond to the text and suggest possible implications: these implications will be dealt with in the following sections, so you do not need to go into any great depth at this stage.

B Two lesson designs

1 Check that the trainees understand the terminology used. Simple glosses could be given, along the lines of:
Presentation: The teacher generates a context, elicits a model sentence and focuses on form and meaning.

Practice: The teacher provides controlled practice. This is usually oral practice.

Production: Learners have the opportunity to use the language in a freer and more communicative context.

Communication: Learners have the opportunity to communicate, using whatever means are available to them.

Language focus: The teacher focuses on the form and meaning of one (or more) language items arising from the communication.

The lesson formats both have a section that introduces new language and both have a practice phase. The main difference is that the second one starts and ends with a communication activity, whereas the first one only ends with one.

2   The teacher is describing the second format.

Communication 1: We started off talking about families. I told the class about my family and then they told each other about theirs in groups.

Language focus: I then wrote 'I've got a *brother*' on the board and they told me words that could replace 'brother'. We practised the pronunciation too.

Practice: We then did a little gap fill that focused on the difference between *have* and *has*.

Communication 2: I then swapped the groups round and they told each other about their families again and this time the listeners tried to draw the family tree of the speaker.

3   The aim of this discussion is for trainees to consider a format that foregrounds fluency in a little more detail. Allow them to work in groups before discussing the issues in open class. You may want to highlight:

   a   False beginner/elementary – on the basis of *have got* being the new language item.

   b   It is often assumed that foregrounding fluency can work only with higher level groups. This example is deliberately chosen to illustrate that it can work at low levels too.

   c   The activity is very similar to that used at the start of the lesson, but the switching around of groups means that the learners are finding out new information. Also, because they repeat the activity after the grammar presentation stage, they should be able to do it more accurately.

   d   It foregrounds the communicative function of language. It credits learners with existing knowledge and encourages them to draw on this capacity. Moreover, the communicative task may trigger a need for specific language items, making their subsequent presentation more relevant and meaningful to the learners. In addition, a lesson that starts with communication tends to be more learner-centred and, ultimately, more motivating, than one that begins with teacher presentation.

   e   It could be argued that the initial phase could 'overrun' and therefore leave less time for the rest of the lesson. Several language needs may become apparent during the initial phase and the teacher may not be able to deal adequately with all of them immediately.

C Task-based learning

For accounts of task-based learning see:

Richards, J. and T. Rodgers (2001) *Approaches and Methods in Language Teaching*, second edition, 223–43 Cambridge University Press.

Willis, D. and J. Willis (2007) *Doing Task-based Teaching*, Oxford University Press.

1   This is a very simple task-based learning model. If you wish, you could build on it by pointing out that in many cases learners may listen or watch expert users of the language perform the task. This acts as a model and learners may notice some of the differences between their

attempts and those of more proficient users of English. You may like to point out that a period of preparation, where learners work individually to think of ideas and necessary language before they start the task, can benefit the way that they eventually perform the task. You could highlight that during the task the learners are probably focusing on fluency, while the reporting phase tends to promote accuracy.

Alternatively, you may prefer to demonstrate a short task cycle.

1   *Communication*: everything up to the point when the teacher puts up a model sentence.
    Language focus: the stage where the teacher highlights the form and meaning of *should*.
    Practice: the stage where the learners complete sentences.
    Communication: the final stage.

2   The teacher could introduce relevant vocabulary at a 'pre-task' phase, e.g. when the teacher introduces the theme of the lesson. Alternatively, the teacher could 'feed in' vocabulary while monitoring the task preparation phase, or by making dictionaries available.

3   There is a 'post-task' phase in which the learners report back on what they did and how they did it.

4   It gives the learners the opportunity to experiment with the new language item(s) and perhaps to see how the new language helps them in achieving the task.

2   The aim of questions 1 and 2 is to demonstrate that the language used in tasks is often predictable to at least some extent and that, therefore, teachers need not be unduly concerned by 'unpredictability' of the language generated.

1   The vocabulary will depend to some extent on what the person did. However, *achieved, succeeded, managed to* and so on may all be useful.

2   If the person is alive, then the present perfect may be used a lot, along with past forms. If the person is dead, then the past forms are likely to predominate. There may also be the need for comparative or superlative structures.

3   The teacher will need to set the task, but also generate some interest in the task, e.g. by talking about someone that they admire. Alternatively, the teacher could initiate a discussion on what makes good/bad role models.

4   The post-task phase will focus on the language used – see 1 and 2, above.

D   Other lesson formats

The aim of this section is to introduce activities where the lesson content and activity flow emerges from, and is driven by, the learners' own needs or interests. The first borrows from the methodology of Community Language Learning (CLL). (For an account of CLL see: Richards, J. & T. Rodgers (2001) *Approaches and Methods in Language Teaching* (second edition) Cambridge University Press, pages 90–99).

1   You may prefer to demonstrate this activity.

1   The activity works well with many classes, including quite large classes.

2   Communication is the driving force of the activity and the language focus highlights language that the learners either needed or used (accurately or not).

3   Learners speak (and therefore listen), and they read and write. They also analyse language after the activity.

4   This comes when the texts are analysed.

2   a   The teacher could take a model sentence from the discussion and check understanding by asking questions (*Did x do y? Would it have been a good idea? Past or present?* etc.). The teacher could highlight the form (*should* + *have* + past participle). To give some practice the teacher

could talk about another situation. *John had a job interview yesterday but he was late. He wore his old jeans ...* etc. and then learners could make sentences in this context using *should(n't) have*. The learners could then talk about mistakes they have made in their lives in small groups.

b The teacher could put some models on the board and check understanding. The learners could then work in groups and discuss advice that they could give the teacher about things such as learning the learners' language, making friends, making more money and so on. Afterwards, they could report back their suggestions to the class.

c The teacher could explain and check new vocabulary (for example, *revision*, *retake*, *cheat* and so on) and then put it on the board and ask learners to discuss exams and assessment they experienced at school.

REFLECTION

1 **Felipe**'s experience is not uncommon. It probably reflects that 'learning' does not equal 'teaching' and it is probably unrealistic to expect learners to be presented with language and to integrate it into their own understanding just 30 minutes or so later. This does not necessarily mean that teaching grammar is a waste of time, but the benefits are likely to be delayed. **Clare** and **Maria** could both be advised to experiment with some of the approaches that have been outlined in the unit.
Dave: when tasks are used a certain amount of language is often predictable and so he may feel more comfortable with this approach than with the other fluency-driven approaches described.

2 Ask trainees to reflect on their teaching practice experience and to consider where substantial communication phases have tended to come in lessons that they have taught.

Optional activity

Adapting coursebooks

The aim of this activity is to encourage trainees to see that they can foreground fluency, while still using coursebooks.

Ask the trainees to look at the coursebook that they are currently using in teaching practice. They should find a grammar point and consider the following questions:

Work in pairs. Look at the coursebook you are using in teaching practice. Find a grammar point and consider the following questions.

a Are there plenty of opportunities to communicate before the grammar presentation?
b If so, might they require the use of the targeted language item(s)?
c If there are not many opportunities to communicate, can you think of an appropriate communication task which links with the theme of the lesson and might provide the opportunity to use the language to be taught?
d Are there plenty of opportunities to communicate after the grammar presentation?
e If not, can you think of an appropriate communication task?

© Cambridge University Press 2007

Allow the trainees to work together, before reporting back their ideas to the class.

19 Planning a scheme of work

Main focus
Planning beyond the individual lesson.

Learning outcomes
1 Trainees understand the principles of selecting and sequencing lessons according to the needs of a group.
2 Trainees are able to analyse schemes of work and see strengths and weaknesses.
3 Trainees are able to produce their own medium-term plan.

Key concepts
- variety, balance, linkage
- sequencing
- review, recycling
- language-focused vs skills-focused lessons

Stage	Focus
A Warm-up	introducing the topic of planning beyond the individual lesson
B Schemes of work	reviewing different types of lessons that may be included in a scheme of work
C Sequencing lessons	trainees analyse a plan, commenting on its strengths and weaknesses
D Lesson planning game	trainees arrange a group of lessons into a logical sequence
Reflection	trainees reflect on what they have learned and put it into practice by planning a sequence of lessons for their learners

A Warm-up

The trainees work in small groups to discuss the complaints and how they could have been avoided. It is likely that all the problems could have been avoided with better planning.

Emiliano: over a period of a course it is usually necessary to build in a variety of material so that lessons do not become overly predictable and eventually boring.

Eriko: language learning does not proceed in a linear way, always going forward. Teachers also need to build in time to practise and revise previously covered material in order to give the learners the best chance of being successful.

Sophie: learners often have a good idea of why they are learning language and what they want to learn. Teachers can find out this information (for example, by using a simple needs analysis) and use it to inform their planning.

Thomas: where two or more teachers share responsibility for a class, it is obviously important that they liaise closely so that lessons fit together appropriately.

Suriya: the teacher could help Suriya simply by telling the class what things they were going to be doing – for example, by putting a plan for the next ten lessons on a noticeboard.

B Schemes of work

Trainees will find it easiest to work with members of the same TP group. Give them some time to discuss the different types of lesson that they have either given or seen, before asking them to report back.

1 and 2 There are no 'correct' answers, as such, and trainees may want to consider how the focus of lessons may shift at different stages. However, the trainees may well suggest that 'systems' lessons, such as those with a grammar or vocabulary focus, tend to have a teacher-fronted focus, at least for part of the time, and that in some classes there is more 'urgency', while in others the pace is more relaxed. The diversity of lesson types will have implications in terms of long-term planning, as it will provide a means for incorporating variety into the scheme of work.

3 Again, there can be no definitive answers as all classes have varying needs and expectations, but suggestions follow.

a There is likely to be a need for quite a lot of reviewing (as the learners have long gaps between lessons). As this is an evening class, you may expect the teacher to build in a lot of fairly relaxed activities. The class will probably be quite learner-centred as it is likely that the teacher will want to maximise the opportunities for the learners to practise using English (they are studying in their own country).

b One may expect to find an emphasis on productive skills (on the basis that the learners are in an English speaking context and should therefore get plenty of reading, and particularly listening, opportunities outside the classroom). There may be a need for quite a lot of social English (ordering food, asking for directions, and so on).

c IELTS has no specific grammar paper but tests all four language skills, so this may encourage teachers to choose a more skills based approach. There are likely to be a number of practice tests and as the stakes are quite high for this class, there is likely to be quite an intensive 'hard-working' atmosphere.

d More than in any other case, the teacher should be able to respond to the needs of the learner. It is likely that the skills required by the learner will be targeted and also the genres of language they need to produce or decode – so for example, there may be a lesson sequence on giving presentations. There is likely to be quite an intensive 'hard-working' atmosphere. The class is unlikely to become teacher-fronted for any length of time.

e Typically early lessons in this context focus on skills work. Receptive skills work may well be apportioned more time, given the level of the learners. Classes may be quite teacher-centred, again, largely because of the level. There will be a need for much social English and also a lot of review work.

C Sequencing lessons

Allow the trainees to work in groups to discuss the timetable and the answers to the questions. The main point for them to see from this activity is that the lessons are more or less randomly placed. With a little more thought, a plan could be developed with a more logical sequence. This section aims to prepare trainees for the planning phase in Section D. There is no need for the trainees to analyse each day in detail. As soon as they have understood the main points (see above) you can move on.

Before they start, ensure the trainees understand that each lesson has a main focus (which is given) but this does not preclude other things happening in the lesson. A grammar lesson may well include some speaking, listening, reading or writing, for example. However, for this activity they should concentrate on the main focus, rather than thinking about how individual lessons may be structured.

1   In terms of quantity in the week, there is probably a reasonable balance between grammar and skills work. It could be argued that there is insufficient vocabulary work (just one lesson) but the teacher could balance this out over other weeks. The problem is in the sequencing, rather than the amount of work in each area over the week.

2   No – Monday has two grammar lessons, while Wednesday has none. Wednesday has three skills lessons but the middle one seems unrelated to the other two. The lessons on Friday contain no obvious links.

3   There is a group of lessons centring around work (Listening – working in a call centre, Speaking – Roleplay – job interviews, Reading – How to do well in a job interview and Speaking – jobs). How to do well in a job interview may link with the grammar lesson on *should* and *must*, which will also link with the lesson on giving advice. The lesson on the present perfect might link to the lesson on writing a news story.

The planning has not exploited these links and some of the sequencing may actually confuse learners. For example, Monday includes revision of the present perfect and this is followed by writing a narrative. This may lead learners to try to use the present perfect in contexts where the past simple or past perfect may be more appropriate.

D Lesson planning game

Divide the trainees into small groups. Cut the lessons up to make cards and give one set of cards to each group. There are four additional cards, which are designed to widen the number of choices that trainees must make. Obviously, there is no single correct answer. However, a possible answer is included below. You may wish to photocopy this and use in the feedback process, with trainees comparing their answer to the one given.

Quiz based on work from this week	Vocabulary – collocations with 'make'	Functional language – asking for advice	Reading/ listening – jigsaw text: husbands and wives	Pronunciation – intonation in questions
Vocabulary – linking words	Speaking and writing – preparing a news story	Listening – a day in the life of an agony aunt	Grammar revision – present perfect simple	Listening – video – a television news bulletin

© Cambridge University Press 2007

Pronunciation – /p/ or /b/?	Writing – writing a narrative	Grammar – second conditional	Functional language – asking for centre directions	Listening – working in a call
Speaking – jobs	Speaking/ vocabulary – money	Vocabulary – describing emotions	Writing – a letter of application	Grammar – uses of 'should' and 'must'
	Speaking – Roleplay – job interviews	Speaking – phobias	Listening – gap filling a song	Reading – How to do well in a job interview

	Monday	Tuesday	Wednesday	Thursday	Friday
09–09.50	Listening – working in a call centre	Grammar – uses of 'should' and 'must'	Functional language – asking for advice	Reading/ listening – jigsaw text: husbands and wives	Speaking/ vocabulary – money
10–10.50	Vocabulary – linking words	Reading – How to do well in a job interview	Listening – a day in the life of an agony aunt	Grammar revision – present perfect simple	Listening – video – a television news bulletin
11–11.50	Speaking – jobs	Pronunciation – intonation in questions	Vocabulary – describing emotions	Vocabulary – collocations with 'make'	Speaking and writing – preparing a news story
12– 12.50	Writing – a letter of application	Speaking – Role play – job interviews	Speaking – phobias	Listening – gap filling a song	Quiz based on work from this week

© Cambridge University Press 2007

> **REFLECTION**
>
> On many CELTA courses, trainees take responsibility for planning their last lessons, with only minimal guidance. You could use this as an opportunity for trainees to plan their final lessons. If so, you will need to ensure that trainees understand the requirements of your centre (length of lessons and so on). It is probably a good idea to get a TP group to outline the main focus of all the lessons the group will teach and to identify the material to be used. You can then check that their ideas are appropriate before allocating lessons to individual trainees to prepare on their own.

20 Motivating learners

Main focus
Ways of maintaining learner motivation.

Learning outcomes
1 Trainees understand and can use a variety of techniques for maintaining learner motivation in the short term.
2 Trainees understand and can use a variety of techniques for maintaining learner motivation in the longer term.

Key concepts
- intrinsic vs extrinsic motivation
- short-term vs long-term motivation
- variety, relevance
- needs, objectives

Stage	Focus
A Warm-up	introducing some reasons for learning a language
B Things teachers can influence	trainees read a text to distinguish between those things that are and are not open to teacher influence
C Ways of influencing motivation	introducing a range of techniques for maintaining motivation
D Adapting material	trainees consider the ways in which material can be adapted to help to maintain motivation
Reflection	trainees complete a review quiz

A Warm-up

1 The key point to be made here is that there are some factors that affect motivation that the teacher can influence and some that are very difficult for the teacher to influence directly. It is worth pointing out that learners in a class will not necessarily all share the same views and be motivated by the same things. If the trainees find the task difficult, you could give them this as the criterion to sort the factors by. However, trainees may think of other interesting criteria by which to divide the items.

Not easily open to influence	Open to influence
The learners know that a good level of English will benefit their career. The learners really like English literature and want to read it in the original language. Learners like socialising with other members of the class.	The learners find the material interesting. The teacher praises and encourages learners. The learners feel the lessons are useful.

2 The trainees can discuss this with other members of their teaching practice group before reporting back to the class.

B Things teachers can influence

1   The questions will be answered by the text, but allow trainees a couple of minutes to discuss the issues as a way into the text.
2   The authors would answer:
    1   Somewhere in between
    2   A routine that is occasionally broken
    3   Probably cooperative (based on their summary of Crookes and Schmidt) although this is hedged slightly in the last paragraph.
    4   No – the last paragraph makes this clear.
3   1   No – first paragraph.
    2   General educational studies.
    3   Generally yes, and presumably this is the view of the authors.
    4   Age and cultural difference – last paragraph.
    5   Answers will vary but stress that the TP session was not necessarily bad if the answers are 'no'. Classes and learners vary in what they want and expect. Also, while activities should be varied, it may not necessarily be appropriate to have lots of different materials in a short space of time, such as one or two lessons.

At this point you may like to review the staging of this section as a possible model of a reading lesson.

C Ways of influencing motivation

The aim of this section is to give some more practical suggestions on maintaining motivation and to give examples for the rather more abstract concepts in B.

You may like to simply discuss each view one at a time in open class. The views of the teachers and learners are **not** in opposition.

1   Suggested answers are below, but may vary according to context.
    Realistic options include:
    • giving work back quickly (if any is collected)
    • encouraging learners
    • testing
    • teaching at an appropriate level
    • displaying work
    • including variety
2   Probably all of these things could be done, although setting personalised objectives may depend on class size and the culture of the institution.
3   Things likely to influence motivation during the course of one lesson include:
    • encouraging learners
    • teaching at an appropriate level
    • including variety
    • using the learners' own material
    • displaying the product of the lesson
4   An argument could be made for all of them impacting on longer term motivation.

D Adapting material

1 It is important to stress that not all activities need adapting to maximise interest. Some learners may like the simplicity of a straightforward activity sometimes. However, variety is important and many activities that appear to lack intrinsic interest can easily be adapted. Ask the trainees to look at the original material and then answer the questions in small groups.

    1 The exercise has been personalised and there is scope for learners to interact and communicate when they compare sentences and perhaps respond to what each other has written

    2 It could be easily turned into a matching game (prepositions with verbs/adjectives).

2 Instead of coursebook characters, the person described could be a real person, e.g. a famous person, or a fellow student. The learner who is guessing could be given a limit to the number of questions they can ask (as in the game '20 questions'), or they could be set a time limit.

3 Allow the trainees to work together and discuss their ideas before reporting back to you.

REFLECTION

You may like to split the group into two. Ask one half of the class to work together. They must help each other and all have the correct answers before they have 'finished'. Ask the other half of the class to work individually and in silence. They must race each other to see who finishes first.

When everyone has finished and you have confirmed the answers, ask the trainees the significance of how you set up the activity – in order to mimic the cooperative/competitive distinction. Make sure they understand though that not all competitive activities are individuals against individuals – group activities can also be competitive.

The clue for 'objectives' could include that they are motivating, can be set for individuals as well as groups and that they can be short or longer term.

1 s	h	o	w	p	r	o	g	r	e	s	s

1. s h o w p r o g r e s s
2. t e s t s
3. e n c o u r a g e m e n t
4. v a r i e t y
5. d i s p l a y w o r k
6. m e e t t h e n e e d s
7. g a m e s

21 Teaching different levels

Main focus
Trainees learn to adapt to teaching different levels.

Learning outcomes
1 Trainees understand the needs of learners at different levels.
2 Trainees understand how skills based lessons may vary at different levels.
3 Trainees understand how lessons with a grammar focus may vary at different levels.

Key concepts
- basic user, independent user, proficient user
- beginner, elementary, pre-intermediate, intermediate, upper-intermediate, advanced
- language grading
- receptive vs productive skills

Stage	Focus
A Warm-up	trainees are introduced to the CEF band descriptors
B Adapting to different levels	trainees consider class management issues at different levels
C Productive skills	trainees consider how productive skills lessons may vary with level
D Receptive skills	trainees consider how receptive skills tasks may vary with level
E Teaching grammar	trainees consider how grammar input may vary with level
Reflection	trainees consider how the issues raised in the unit will impact on their own teaching

This unit could usefully be done at the time when trainees switch to teaching different levels. You could replace the sample material given here with material from books trainees are using in teaching practice. The final (Reflection) section is intended to give fairly concrete and practical advice on adapting to a class, as trainees move from one level to another.

A Warm-up

1 and 2 CEF levels

> Can express him/herself fluently and spontaneously without much obvious searching for expressions. Can use language flexibly and effectively for social, academic and professional purposes. Can produce clear, well-structured, detailed text on complex subjects. **C1**
>
> Can interact with a degree of fluency and spontaneity that makes regular interaction with native speakers quite possible without strain for either party. Can produce clear, detailed text on a wide range of subjects and explain a viewpoint on a topical issue giving the advantages and disadvantages of different options. **B2**
>
> Can deal with most situations likely to arise whilst travelling in an area where the language is spoken. Can produce simple connected text on topics which are familiar or of personal interest. Can describe experiences and events, dreams, hopes and ambitions and briefly give reasons and explanations for opinions and plans. **B1**
>
> Can understand sentences and frequently used expressions related to areas of most immediate relevance ... Can communicate in simple and routine tasks requiring a simple and direct exchange of information on familiar and routine matters. **A2**
>
> Can understand and use familiar everyday expressions and very basic phrases aimed at the satisfaction of needs of a concrete type ... Can interact in a simple way provided the other person talks slowly and clearly and is prepared to help. **A1**

You may want to relate these CEF levels to the names of the levels that trainees are teaching and observing, and which are customarily used in labelling coursebooks, e.g. advanced (C1), upper-intermediate (B2), intermediate (B1), pre-intermediate (A2), elementary/beginner (A1).

The descriptor for C2 was not included in the task, as this is a level that is rarely encountered by most teachers, apart from those teaching ESP or Proficiency classes. For reference, here is the descriptor for C2:

> Can understand with ease virtually everything heard or read. Can summarise information from different written and spoken sources, reconstructing arguments and accounts in a coherent presentation. Can express him/herself spontaneously, very fluently and precisely, differentiating finer shades of meaning even in more complex situations.

3 The aim of this section is for trainees to apply the descriptors to themselves, and to assess their usefulness/accuracy.

4 The aim of this section is to get trainees thinking about how language level affects the needs of learners. You may prefer to dictate the sentence stems without having the trainees open their books. This would help to create a group atmosphere rather than having the trainees read and write individually, with each person working at their own pace.

B Adapting to different levels

1   Allow the trainees a few moments to read the statements and make their choices. They should find this relatively easy.

Rachel, elementary to upper-intermediate, statements: a, b, f.

Tom, upper-intermediate to elementary, statements: c, d, e, g.

You may wish to highlight that at lower levels teachers need to work much harder at grading their language appropriately. Also, at lower levels, learners often need more thorough preparation for tasks. At higher levels teachers may need a greater degree of language awareness as explanations become more sophisticated and distinctions more subtle.

2   Again, this should be very straightforward. The aim is simply to help trainees to see the link between these issues and their own teaching practice.

C Productive skills

1   Allow the trainees to read the first piece of material with a partner.
  1   The learners prepare part of the exchange by writing questions.
  2   The exchanges in part 3 are fairly predictable – at least to the extent that they are likely to be characterised by just one turn for each learner before the next question is asked, so the exchanges are very short. The important thing to emphasise is that at lower levels learners often need a greater amount of preparation before a speaking exercise and even then exchanges may be quite short.
2   Again trainees could discuss this in groups before reporting back to you in open class. They may suggest that learners are more capable of producing language spontaneously and are able to extend speaking activities with more turns and longer exchanges. After reading the extract, trainees may point out that there is less preparation built into the activity. The learners have to talk about a range of topics (unlike in the first example) and that they are invited to ask each other an unspecified number of questions (rather than just one).
3   At higher levels writing tasks may be longer. There may be a greater focus on the beyond sentence level characteristics of the text (linking and so on). There may be instruction in different genres of writing (types of letter, CVs and so on). Learners may respond to input data (such as having to write a letter of reply) and the input may be longer and more sophisticated than at lower levels. At lower levels there may be a greater focus on sentence level writing. Where a longer text is produced, learners are likely to need a greater amount of support – for example, the use of a parallel text.

D Receptive skills

1   The text was originally published in an intermediate coursebook. Trainees may comment on the length of the text, and its ungraded nature, including its use of relatively low frequency vocabulary and the inclusion of features of spoken language that suggest it was unscripted. However, as the next task shows, this does not mean that it could not be used at lower levels.
2   Allow the trainees some time to work in small groups to discuss their ideas before reporting back to you.
    Lesson a, advanced: there is no pre-teaching; the learners are 'plunged' into the text and have to listen closely in order to infer what the text is about, using a combination of 'top-down' and 'bottom-up' clues.

Lesson b, elementary: the learners are 'positioned' as close as possible to the gist of the text with pictures, and the task is a very general one – all they have to do is recognise key words like *bridge, jumped, river*; they can also collaborate in solving the task, and are given the extra help of the written transcript.

Lesson c, intermediate: the learners are set a gist task, which helps them focus on the main details of the text, before further details are extracted; the sequence moves from reception to (more challenging) production.

3   It is important for trainees to realise that 'level' is not just about the text chosen. It is about the combination of text and task. Tasks can be used to modify the level of difficulty. Look, for example, at how much more support the learners in c get with decoding the text than those in a.

E   Teaching grammar

1   Allow the trainees some time to consider the question in small groups before reporting back. If the following points are not raised, you may like to point out that at higher levels context may be generated through, for example, a fairly long text – but at lower levels this would place too great a burden. Rules typically become more sophisticated and frequently new language is contrasted with existing knowledge. It is often assumed that learners have a better understanding of metalanguage at higher levels. More than one form may be presented at one time at higher levels, but this is less likely at lower levels. Practice activities are frequently more extended at higher levels.

2   At this point it may be worth pointing out that the fundamental principles of teaching are not altered. Learners still need to know about form and meaning and the contexts in which new language items can be used.

3   Allow the trainees some time to read the material. Make sure that they notice that extract 1 (*Inside Out*) is upper-intermediate level and extract 2 (*Innovations*) is pre-intermediate. They should see that at the lower level the present perfect simple is introduced on its own, but at the higher level it is contrasted with the continuous form. The lower level material also pays more attention to form (irregular past participle forms and word order, for example) whereas this is assumed to be known at the higher level. They should also be able to see that the rules have become more sophisticated at the higher level.

REFLECTION

The aim of this section is for the trainees to think about their classes and be able to pass on useful information to another inexperienced teacher. Tell trainees that they can add additional bullet points, or indeed, leave some blank. They should consider how the level of the class affects management (e.g. grading language), the teaching of skills and systems and so on. You could suggest that in the box marked 'Other issues' they think of other useful information that is not directly related to level – the needs and preferences of individual learners, for example.

22 English for Special Purposes

Main focus

To learn how to adapt classroom teaching to the needs of specific groups or types of learners, e.g. business, one-to-one.

Learning outcomes

- Trainees understand the main differences between teaching ESP and teaching general English.
- Trainees understand how ESP courses are planned, taught, and assessed.
- Trainees understand some principles of effective one-to-one teaching.

Key concepts

- English for Special Purposes; English for Academic Purposes
- business English
- one-to-one teaching
- needs analysis
- text analysis
- competencies

Stage	Focus
A Warm-up	doing a 'find someone who' activity
B Special purposes	identifying ESP vs general English contexts
C Needs analysis	designing a simple questionnaire
D Text analysis	analysing the discourse needs of a target ESP cohort
E Materials	identifying the distinctive features of ESP materials
F One-to-one	exploring methodological issues related to one-to-one teaching
G Assessment	ranking competency statements, and devising testing procedures
Reflection	reflecting on some of the key issues related to ESP teaching

A Warm-up

The point of this activity (apart from demonstrating a popular activity type) is to identify possible specialist fields that the trainees might have knowledge of, or experience in, and which could qualify them to teach an ESP subject. At the same time, as pointed out below, lack of such knowledge does not necessarily disqualify teachers from teaching ESP.

B Special purposes

1 Make sure trainees understand the difference between ESP and general English.

English for Special (or Specific) Purposes (ESP)	General English
a c e f	b d g

Note that f) can also be classified as EAP (*English for Academic Purposes*). a), c), e) and f) are clearly ESP situations; b) is a general English exam class; d) could possibly be considered as ESP, although 'social English' is as much a component of general English courses as business English ones; g) might possibly include some ESP elements, but given the level (beginners) and the job diversity, it is unlikely to be highly specific.

2 1 The point of this question is to defuse anxiety as to the extent of specialist knowledge needed in order to teach ESP. None of the ESP situations would necessarily require extensive specialist knowledge in the learner's subject, assuming that relevant materials were available, and that the learner's discourse needs had been identified (see below on *needs analysis* and *text analysis*). In a), for example, the focus is less on the subject area than on the presentation skills; in c), knowledge of what air traffic controllers are required to do and say would be important, plus example exchanges in a variety of situations; in d), knowledge of the kinds of social situations that occur at trade fairs would be an advantage; in e), some business experience, and in f), some academic background would be an advantage. But, essentially, the ESP teacher needs access to the kinds of texts and discourses that the student has to be competent in, rather than any extensive specialist knowledge. Point out that in many ESP contexts it is enough to show interest in the subject, and to be able to ask intelligent questions about it.

2 Situations a), d) and e) are one-to-one (see below).

C Needs analysis

1 Questions should focus on the *what*, *why*, *how* and *who* of the English that is used in the job. (You may want to write these question words on the board as prompts.) i.e. what are the topics that are dealt with (the *field*), for what purposes, in what *mode* (i.e., speaking, reading, etc.), and with whom, including with what degree of formality (the *tenor*)? Some typical questions might be:

- What topics do you need to communicate about?
- What functions do you use (e.g., giving instructions, making requests, etc.)
- What level of accuracy is required?
- Do you use English only for technical purposes, or also for social purposes?
- Do you have to speak – if so, do you speak face-to-face, or by phone etc.? Do you speak to one person or several?
- Is there a 'script' that you follow?
- Do you have to read and write? If so, what?
- Are there models for the documents that you have to produce?
- Do you communicate with mainly native speakers, or with other non-native speakers?
- What is their rank and social distance, relative to you?

D Text analysis

Note: A *discourse community* is any group of people who share a common interest, profession, academic field, or hobby, and who talk or write about it using conventions of language (such as technical terms) that are understood by that community, but which may be obscure to those who are not part of the community.

1 The style is impersonal and formal, with longer Latinate words (eg *verify, examined, located*) in preference to short, Anglo-Saxon ones (e.g. *check(ed), found*). There are a number of technical terms and many of these take the form of long noun phrases (*watertight door systems, electrically operated watertight doors, the local control switch*, etc.). This makes the text lexically dense (i.e. there is a high proportion of content words to function words). There are a number of modal verbs, expressing obligation (*shall, should*) and probability (*may*). There are several passive constructions: *should be examined, may be caused*, etc.

2 Again, the style is impersonal, with a preponderance of formal and technical language, and the use of the passive, but with shorter, less complex and less dense sentences than the text from the manual, and with ellipsis (omission) of pronouns, as in *[I] examined …[I] visited …* Note also the frequent use of *satisfactory/satisfactorily*, including the collocation *found satisfactory*; also the word families *inspect/inspection* and *examine/examination*.

3 Presumably, the inspector would have needed to make requests, such as *Could you open the pressure valves, please? Can I see the plans?* as well as to ask questions such as *Why is this not working/missing/not finished?* etc.

4 Classroom tasks might include: reading sections of the manual, and using these as a prompt for asking questions; identifying on a diagram or picture features that are mentioned in the manual; listening to a recording of an inspection; role playing an inspection, including making requests; writing reports in the appropriate style.

E Materials

1 The material is designed for teaching the language of business.
2 It differs from general English mainly in its topic, as realised in the choice of vocabulary (*sales, turnover, market, bank interest rates*, etc.).
3 It is similar in: its choice of tasks (matching, sentence completion, personalisation), the progression from an awareness-raising activity, through controlled practice to freer practice and its focus on discrete items of grammar and their uses (past simple; present perfect).

F One-to-one

1 Explain that ESP teaching is sometimes conducted on a one-to-one basis. Ask trainees to think about the advantages and disadvantages.

Advantages	Disadvantages
• teacher can tailor instruction to learner's needs, learning style, pace, level, etc. • learner can be involved in choosing course content, and providing materials • learner gets teacher's undivided attention • learner's practice opportunities are maximised • likely to be more motivating for the learner	• only interaction is with teacher – no pair/groupwork with other learners • intensive, potentially tiring • difficult to plan lessons around a coursebook, which tends to be written for groups

2 The negative factors can be countered by: (a) varying the interactional focus, e.g. by setting up roleplays or information gap activities in which the teacher takes part, and then reversing roles; (b) if possible, changing the focus by leaving the class and going somewhere else together, e.g. a library, café, or shopping centre; (c) encouraging the learner to bring to the class texts that are relevant to their specific needs, e.g. business letters, emails, catalogues, and using these as the content of the lesson.

G Assessment

Explain that assessment of ESP students often takes the form of identifying and testing specific *competencies*. These often take the form of *'can do' statements*.

1 The order is: c (ALTE Breakthrough Level); f (Level 1); a (Level 2); e (Level 3); b (Level 4); d (Level 5).

2 This competency could be tested by recording a number of typical messages, which the learners take down and then either report back to the examiner, or record as voicemail messages.

REFLECTION

1 Points that might emerge from this discussion are:
   a Many ESP teachers will agree with this statement, while at the same time noting that ESP learners can be quite demanding, since they have a clearer idea of their needs than do most general English learners.
   b Subject knowledge certainly helps, and many would consider it a prerequisite, but in reality it is not always possible. ESP teachers are often able to exploit the knowledge their learners have (e.g., by getting them to *teach* the teacher or other students), while providing the necessary language support.
   c This is generally the case, although sometimes even beginners can be given ESP instruction, especially with regard to the vocabulary content of their courses. But most ESP teaching is targeted at learners who are at an intermediate level or above.
   d In an ideal world, this might be the case – where first the students' needs are analysed and then courses are designed to meet those needs. But even where such an ESP-ish approach is not possible, most experienced teachers are sensitive to their students' particular needs and tend to individualise their teaching accordingly.
2 This question links back to the warm-up activity at the beginning of the session. Invite trainees to talk about their own specialisms or interests, and discuss whether – and how – these could form the basis of a course. For example, trainees may have previous training or experience in areas of business or technology. Or they may have a particular hobby or interest. Point out the likelihood of there being someone, somewhere, who shares the same background and needs to be able to communicate about it in English.

23 Teaching literacy

<table>
<tr><td>

Main focus

Ways of developing basic and functional literacy.

Learning outcomes

1 Trainees understand the principal ways of developing basic reading and writing skills.
2 Trainees understand some teaching implications of the notion of functional literacy.

</td><td>

Key concepts

- literacy, illiteracy; functional literacy
- reading, writing, spelling, script
- first language, second language
- genre
- ESL

</td></tr>
</table>

Stage	Focus
A Warm-up	defining literacy
B L1 and L2 literacy	introducing typical profiles of learners who may have literacy needs
C Lessons from learners	practical tips on conducting reading and writing classes with learners with literacy needs
D Reading activities	introducing a range of reading activities, appropriate for learners with literacy needs
E Writing activities	introducing a range of writing activities, appropriate for learners with literacy needs
F Functional literacy	introducing an approach to the teaching of specific genres of writing
Reflection	trainees review key points in teaching learners with literacy needs

Developing reading skills is dealt with in Unit 11.
Developing writing skills is dealt with in Unit 14.

There is one optional activity that supports the unit. It highlights potential difficulties that learners may have when learning to write.

A Warm-up

You could start this section by asking the trainees themselves to define literacy. They can then read the text. Note that literacy, as defined here, is more than simply the ability to read and write; it entails knowing how to function actively in the target culture, as a reader and writer of that culture's texts. As such, the concept of literacy is particularly relevant to ESL (English as a second language) learners.

1 Trainees should be able to come up with a variety of text types, many of which will be bureaucratic in nature, e.g. applying for asylum seeker status, reading a housing contract, filling in a medical history form, etc.

2 The main difference between 'doing reading and writing' and teaching for functional literacy is the nature and purpose of the texts, and the fact that many learners may lack basic literacy in their first language.

B L1 and L2 literacy

1 Aasmah is literate in her first language, but not in English; Halima is neither literate in her first language nor in English; Huseyin is literate in his first languages and, to a certain extent in English, but lacks functional literacy.

2 The important point to make is that learners who have problems with literacy could have speaking and listening skills at any level from beginner to advanced. Therefore it is difficult to speak of an overall level for Aasmah and Halima because their abilities in each skill are so uneven.

3 Reading and writing are often used to create contexts, give practice, create records of new language items and so on.

4 Aasmah is literate in her own language and this may help her in becoming literate in English. She may be familiar with certain text types and their organisation (although this can vary with culture). She will be familiar with the sort of information available in a dictionary and will be able to use a bi-lingual dictionary. She will know how to hold a pen, and probably how to use a keyboard, as well as perhaps knowing how to exploit spell checkers and so on. On the other hand, it's worth pointing out that she may not be familiar with Roman script and its conventions, such as capitalisation, punctuation and so on.

5 Huseyin needs to be able to read and write connected text, and often texts that are of a rather formal register; the ability to write isolated sentences does not necessarily prepare him for his specific needs.

6 He needs to be familiar with the specific genres that he will encounter, and the way that the register of these genres is sensitive to such context factors as the relationship between writers and readers.

C Lessons from learners

This section gives some practical tips on the needs of learners. Allow the trainees to think individually before comparing with each other and then confirming ideas in open class. If time is short, you can allocate different 'case studies' to different pairs or groups of trainees.

Karim: At low levels of reading ability it is generally considered good practice to use large fonts and to put little on the page.

Soula: Teachers need to stay patient and be very encouraging.

Li Na: Learners need bottom-up strategies (letter/sound relations) but this can be integrated with a 'top-down' approach, at least for some words, particularly those that are very frequent and familiar. It could be pointed out that context (including co-text) may be one thing that helps in the decoding process and this may make simple sentences and texts relatively easier than some individual words.

Shireen: Teachers need to teach reading skills based on language that is already known to the learners orally.

Ali: Fatigue is a factor. Writing activities need to be short at this level and learners will need breaks.

Samia: Learners who have literacy needs are unlikely to be able to copy things from the board quickly and efficiently. Teachers may need to consider putting more on handouts so that learners get a written record of the key points of the lesson.

Hussein: Some learners, particularly those who are not literate in their own language, will need help with things that may seem obvious to a teacher and can therefore be overlooked.

Mei Yan: Even copying can be difficult for learners with literacy needs because there is a limit to what can be stored in 'working memory' – causing delays as they need to constantly look for the next part.

D Reading activities

The main point of this section is to give the trainees a set of reading activities that would be appropriate at very low levels of reading ability. You may like to spend some time ensuring that they understand how each activity works, perhaps demonstrating some of them.

1 Trainees could work in pairs before reporting back their ideas.

word level	sentence level	text level
Reading bingo Odd one out Matching	Describing pictures	Find and underline Ordering Next word

E Writing activities

Again, the key point of this section is to give the trainees a set of writing activities that would be appropriate at very low levels of writing ability.

You may like to spend some time ensuring that trainees understand how each activity works, perhaps demonstrating some of them. If you prefer, or are short of time, you could write 'spelling', 'letter formation' and 'sentence formation' on the board and ask the trainees to match the activities to the headings.

a) and f) both practise spelling
b) and e) both practise the mechanical formation of letters
c) and d) both practise sentence level writing

F Functional literacy

Assuming trainees have already covered Unit 14: Developing writing skills, ask them to refer back to the coursebook extract in C2 of that unit, as a point of comparison.

1 The material is similar to general English writing exercises, in that it adopts a staged approach to the teaching of writing, but is perhaps different in that it foregrounds a model text which is subject to analysis in terms of its overall organisation (its 'macrostructure') – on the assumption, no doubt, that this macrostructure is generic. Also, the utilitarian nature of the text perhaps contrasts with more discursive or expressive text types found in general English courses.

2 This question links back to the warm-up task, where trainees brainstormed the challenges facing new arrivals in an English-speaking culture. Trainees should be encouraged to think of

not just 'paper' text types, but digital texts as well, such as internet websites, email correspondence, and text-messaging. Any text type that has a generic structure (i.e. one that can be used as a model for the generation of specific texts) lends itself to this model-driven approach.

REFLECTION

You may prefer to reproduce the diagram on large pieces of paper and have the trainees make a poster. Alternatively, you could make it a whole group activity with trainees writing on the board. Among the points that the trainees could make are the following:

reading	reading and writing	writing
• Use large fonts. • Don't put too much on a page. • Practise reading single words, sentences and short texts.	• Be patient. • Work with 'known' language. • Remember that learners get tired very quickly. • Introduce learners to particular genres. • Use models.	• Allow lots of time. • Practise forming letters, spelling, and handwriting. • Ask learners to produce sentences and short texts.

Optional activity

Learning to write

Identify the difficulties illustrated by these pieces of writing.

he lives in london his father and his fathers father are also there

My doctor says anapple aday is goodfor you.

I have a coff so I am eating a lot of froot.

I have lot of difficulty when I try to write in English

Trainer's notes

Trainees could work in small groups before reporting back their ideas.

1 This demonstrates the need for learners to use punctuation appropriately, particularly capital letters and full stops. (You may like to point out that readers also have to understand the significance of punctuation.)

2 As learners try to put into writing the words that they speak, they have to become aware of word boundaries and the need to use spacing appropriately.

3 This demonstrates that there are sound/spelling irregularities in English and these can cause problems for learners trying to write.

4 This demonstrates the need for learners to master the 'mechanics' of handwriting – the formation of letters, words and sentences.

24 Monitoring and assessing learning

Main focus	**Key concepts**
Ways of monitoring and assessing learning.	• placement, diagnostic, progress and achievement tests

Main focus

Ways of monitoring and assessing learning.

Learning outcomes

1 Trainees understand some of the main reasons for testing learners.
2 Trainees understand a variety of question types.
3 Trainees can use their understanding to design a short progress test for a given group of learners.

Key concepts

- placement, diagnostic, progress and achievement tests
- discrete-item vs integrated tests
- language knowledge vs language use
- reliability: objectivity vs subjectivity
- validity
- review, recycling
- self-assessment

Stage	Focus
A Warm-up	trainees do a short test
B Reasons to test learners	introducing trainees to common reasons for using tests
C Ways of testing	introducing common question types
D How not to test	introducing some basic principles of test design
E Analysing a test	trainees analyse a progress test
F Other ways of monitoring progress	trainees are introduced to alternatives to testing for monitoring progress
Reflection	trainees put what they have learned into practice by designing a short test

A Warm-up

Trainees do a short test, based on a very small proportion of the CELTA course. Later in the unit they have a chance to reflect on the test so there is no need to go into a lot of detail here about how the test is designed. You may like to have the trainees work individually, but they could, alternatively, work collaboratively. Suggested answers:

1 *will* + *be* + *-ing*
2 a) I'm meeting b) will buy c) will win
3 form (spoken and written), meaning, collocation, degree of formality, grammatical restrictions of use, etc.
4 Is the speaker walking to the shop now? (no) Will he go in the future? (yes) Has he already decided to go? (yes)
5 Set achievable objectives, plan lessons that have variety, select interesting and relevant material, etc.

B Reasons to test learners

1. a for placement purposes
   b for diagnostic purposes – this is essentially forward looking and helps the teacher plan a relevant and useful sequence of lessons.
   c to check progress – this is essentially backward looking at things that have already been covered.
   d to assess achievement over the entire course – similar to c) but over a longer period.
2. As well as the reasons listed above, tests are often used to fit in with learner expectations, to screen for entry to public exams or to help prepare for public exams. The main drawback is that if tests are over-used they can end up replacing teaching.

C Ways of testing

1. Ensure that trainees understand the terms used in the questions.
   a individual (discrete) language items: Although multiple-choice questions can be used to assess a range of language, each item is discrete. Sentence transformations also tend to test individual language items, as would the sentence production exercise. Gap-fill exercises can be used to test one language point (if, for example, only auxiliary verbs are removed) but can be used to test a range of language.
   b language items in combination: Direct tests of productive skills (writing a composition and learners describing pictures) will involve integrated language.
   c and d language knowledge/language use: To some extent this will depend on exactly how the task is used. The example given of sentence production would be language in use (the learners write things that are meaningful and communicate something about themselves). Oral interviews may well do the same, although simply describing a picture (for no obvious reason) is more a test of language knowledge. Describing pictures to find differences between them, for example, would be language use. Depending on the precise task, the composition may also be a test of language use.
   e objective marking: Multiple-choice questions, gap-fill exercises and matching text will be marked objectively. The sentence transformations will also be fairly objective, but judgements about acceptability may have to be made in some cases, and the same is true for the sentence production exercise.
   f subjective marking: Direct tests of productive skills (writing a composition and learners describing pictures) will involve some degree of subjectivity in the marking and will therefore require assessment criteria so that performance can be graded with some degree of consistency.
2. You may like to assign groups to look at the different areas to ensure that they are all covered. The table below shows probable answers, although arguments for alternatives could be made. Virtually everything will involve vocabulary and grammar to some extent, and the brackets indicate where something is tested but is not the primary focus. Multiple-choice questions can be used to test writing skills indirectly (for example by choosing the most appropriate linking word).

Test types	receptive skills	productive skills	vocabulary and grammar
Multiple-choice questions	✓	(✓)	✓
Gap-fill exercises	✓		✓
Sentence transformations		(✓)	✓
Writing a composition		✓	(✓)
Oral interviews		✓	(✓)
Matching	✓		(✓)
Sentence production		✓	✓

3 Trainees may identify points such as:

Success at communicating, which may be influenced by:
- fluency – the ability to keep going and get the message across
- accuracy of language production, including prosodic features of pronunciation and individual sounds
- range of vocabulary and structures used
- strategies for dealing with communication breakdowns

Trainees will then need to further break these down for their criteria. For example:

	A Fully able to communicate intended meaning	B Able to communicate most of intended meaning	C Unable to communicate significant parts of intended meaning
Range of vocabulary and structures	A good range of vocabulary and structures	An adequate range of vocabulary and structures	An inadequate range of vocabulary and structures to communicate effectively
Fluency	Little unnatural hesitation	Noticeable pausing and hesitation	Pausing and hesitation put an undue burden on the listener
Accuracy (including pronunciation)	Few noticeable errors	Some errors but rarely interfere with meaning	A number of errors, some of which interfere with meaning
Communication strategies	Can repair breakdowns in communication	Can repair breakdowns in communication for the most part	Unable to repair breakdowns in communication

4 Of course, criteria will vary with level and trainees may devise criteria with more than three points on the scale. Trainees may argue that a mark should be given for each item, or that a single mark is awarded on a 'best-fit' basis. This task may take some time. You may prefer to assign two or three areas to each group, rather than ask all groups to do all categories. Alternatively, you could do one on the board in open class to serve as a model.

D How not to test

Allow the trainees a few minutes to complete their sentences before comparing with each other. Answers will vary but possible answers are:

a Instructions need to be clear. (Examples are useful to achieve this.)

b The content of the test should reflect the content of the course.

c Feedback should be constructive.

E Analysing a test

1 The aim of this section is to reinforce the need for 'content validity'. It is reasonable to assume that what is tested is representative of what has been taught.

Section 1 tests modality.   Section 4 tests prepositions.

Section 2 tests vocabulary.   Section 5 tests vocabulary – phrases with 'do'.

Section 3 tests pronunciation   Section 6 tests linking words.
   (a range of vowel sounds).

2 1 It is designed as an informal test.

   2 Learners could do it in pairs or groups.

   3 Answers will vary.

   4 Answers will vary.

F Other ways of monitoring progress

1 Shaun: teacher; Laura and Kirsty: the learners assess themselves.

2 All the ideas are intended to be practical for most contexts.

Answers to 3 and 4 will vary.

REFLECTION

1 a One of the reasons for testing is to encourage learners to look back at what they have done and revise it – so it can be useful to tell learners that a test is coming up. Recycling language is important and tests, however small and informal, are an easy way of achieving that.

  b Testing in a classroom doesn't have to be formal. Learners could do things in pairs or groups.

  c In the case of progress tests everything is a kind of preparation. It is sometimes a good idea to spend a lesson or two looking back and consolidating what has been done.

  d Testing typically deals with 'right' and 'wrong'. Teaching deals with understanding and therefore an error, for example, is seen as something that could lead to development and greater understanding, whereas in testing it is 'punished'. Teaching is concerned with development, whereas testing deals with current knowledge.

2 There are issues of 'content validity'. The CELTA course is very practical in nature and classroom based, so a written test is dubious. Of course, in such a short test it is difficult to include a representative sample of work, and here there is a lot on future forms and little on other language areas studied. Trainees may also discuss issues of timing, mark allocation per question and so on.

3 If time is short this could be reduced to identifying appropriate content and question types.

25 Teaching exam classes

> **Main focus**
> To learn how to adapt classroom teaching to the needs of groups preparing for exams.
>
> **Learning outcomes**
> 1 Trainees know some basic information about a range of public exams.
> 2 Trainees understand some basic principles of teaching exam classes.
>
> **Key concepts**
> - types of public exams, levels of public exams
> - mock tests
> - key word transformations, picture discussion, transactional writing, text completion

Stage	Focus
A Warm-up	introducing some popular ELT exams
B Teaching exam classes	a text completion activity, giving practical advice on dealing with exam classes
C Exam question types	introducing common exam question types
D Exam materials	trainees analyse exam focused materials
Reflection	trainees reflect on what they have learned by creating and using a sentence completion task

There is one optional activity that supports the unit, in which trainees analyse some IELTS preparation material.

A Warm-up

1 Ask the trainees to memorise as much as they can of the table in 90 seconds. After 90 seconds tell them to close their books. Ask them a question, such as *What does CAE stand for?* Trainees work in pairs. They ask and answer similar questions swapping roles after about one minute. You may need to allow the questioners to consult their books.
2 Allow trainees time to prepare some questions. Either direct them to the internet to find answers, or answer as many as you can yourself. Don't worry if you cannot answer all of the questions. You may like to point out other sources of potential information, such as:
   - asking an experienced teacher
   - looking in a preparation book
   - contacting the exam board
   - searching on the internet

B Teaching exam classes

The aim here is for trainees to experience a common exam question format while also gaining some tips on teaching exam classes.

1 The trainees should try completing the text individually. They can then compare their answers with a partner before confirming these in open class with you.
 Answers: 1–c) 2–e) 3–a) 4–d). (Sentence b is not used.)

2 Trainees may make different arguments depending on the amount of detail they feel should be included, but overall the sentences give a reasonable summary of the key points. You may like to reinforce the importance of these tips for newly qualified teachers taking on the responsibility of teaching exam classes.

3 This is a text completion exercise, a task type used in several public examinations. It tests reading skills, particularly the recognition of text organisation. It is not a particularly authentic task and may therefore be of limited value to non-exam students if they cannot see the point of it and may lead some candidates to wonder why they are asked to do something in an exam that they will not have to do in real life.

C Exam question types

This section follows on from the text completion task.

1 and 2 Make sure the trainees understand how the activities work. Ask the trainees to discuss their answers in small groups before they report back in open class. Encourage them to expand on their answers – rather than saying 'writing skills', for example, see if they can recognise the text type generated and the skills a candidate would need to produce it. You may like to make the following points:

a Key word transformations
 • typically used to test grammar/vocabulary
 • sometimes used to practise a particular structure (for example, active to passive) but mainly used as a testing device

b Picture discussion
 • speaking skills, including turn-taking and organising discourse
 • listening skills also required
 • pictures can be a useful prompt in many classes

c Transactional writing
 • writing skills – informal emails
 • language of giving advice
 • writing emails to friends may be a fairly common need – and therefore may be useful

D Exam materials

For this section you will need one or more exam-focused coursebooks and enough copies to distribute to the class.

Trainees could work in small groups, each group analysing a different book. It is important for the trainees to recognise that the books will be a support to them and that there will be material that they can use and adapt as in any other coursebook. This will make the teaching of exam classes less daunting. It is also helpful if trainees can identify the activities that are very exam focused.

You could replace this activity with the optional activity below, if you wish.

Explain the activity to the trainees, allow time for them to create their sentences and sentence stems before giving them to their partner. Have a brief reporting back phase, summarising the main points.

Optional activity

Look at the extracts below and answer the questions.

1 In extract (a), what is the purpose of the note?
2 Which extract aims to improve the learning skills of the learner?
3 Two of the extracts are extremely similar to specific exam tasks. Which two, do you think?
4 How might you support learners doing extracts (a), (b) and (c), before, during or after the tasks?
5 Would you give such support throughout the entire course?

a

note

In summary completion tasks you may be given a list of words to choose from. These will usually belong to the same word class, for example nouns.

Questions 7–10: Summary completion
Complete the summary below using words from the list.

accuracy   democracy   neutrality
vandalism   interest   originality
reputations   quality

Criticism of Wikipedia has focused on the question of (7).................. . Some contributors are registered with the site, and over time they are able to improve their (8).................. . There are also administrators who carry out checks on entries and prevent (9).................. . Other policies to maintain high standards include a rule that entries should aim at (10).................. in writing style.

b

1 Discuss these questions.

Money
How do you think developments in information technology will alter the way individuals deal with their money in the future?
How do you predict people's shopping habits will change in the future?

c

Language for writing

1 Which of the adverbs and adverb phrases given could be used to complete sentences a–f?

a The situation today is .... different from that of just a few years ago.
   completely   strongly   vastly

b Our investigations proved .... that improvements have occurred.
   conclusively   definitively   doubtlessly

c There is a .... significant association between achievement and social background.
   greatly   highly   statistically

d Computer ownership rose .... during the 1990s.
  distinctly   rapidly   sharply

e The price of petrol went up by ten per cent last year. ...., people used their cars less frequently.
  Amazingly   Not surprisingly   Probably

f Research has .... shown that exposure to loud noise can ....
  damage our hearing.
  clearly   evidently   consistently
  dangerously   seriously   severely

d

IELTS to do list

Choose one of the following to do outside class.

Where to look

www.oup.com/elt/ielts

☐ Think of something you normally do on the Internet in your own language and do it in English instead.

☐ Compare the way a big story is covered on different news websites, e.g. 'serious' and 'popular', 'left' and 'right', UK and US.

☐ Choose a topic from this book, such as a writing task you have to do. Research the topic using key words. Ask yourself whether this helped you come up with new ideas.

☐ Follow the links on the OUP website (www.oup.com/elt/ielts) to sources of IELTS-style materials. Bookmark the most interesting websites, and go back to them frequently.

IELTS Masterclass Haines/May

Trainer's notes for optional activity

The trainees could work in small groups to answer the questions. Point out that the first piece of material (the summary) comes after a listening text.

1 In extract (a) the purpose of the note is to give additional information about the question type that the learners could expect in the exam. It is part of training for the exam.

2 The final extract aims to improve the learning skills of the learner. You may like to point out that these tasks would also be useful for learners who are not preparing for exams.

3 The summary and the speaking task are very close to tasks that candidates have to do in the exam. The gap fill is actually designed to develop writing skills, which are not tested in this way in the exam.

4 The aim of this question is to get trainees to think about the differences between 'teaching' and 'testing'. 'Teaching' may involve learners making predictions about texts and what they'll read/listen to, breaking an audio recording into more manageable segments, allowing learners to discuss answers before reporting back to the teacher and so on. Necessary vocabulary may be pre-taught (for example, to support the writing gap fill). 'Testing' would be more likely to involve doing the activities simply as they stand. There is likely to be a lot of support at the beginning. By the end of the course, learners will need to have some practice in more exam-like conditions and so some support may have to be withdrawn.

26 Choosing and using teaching resources

Main focus

To raise awareness about the range of resources available and how these can be best exploited.

Learning outcomes

- Trainees know how to select and evaluate coursebooks and other resources.
- Trainees are aware of the need to adapt and supplement materials where appropriate.
- Trainees appreciate the contribution of technology to learning and also know how to cope without it.

Key concepts

- coursebooks, workbooks, etc.
- supplementary materials
- selecting, adapting and supplementing materials
- technology and aids
- teaching without technology

Stage	Focus
A Warm-up	choosing resources to take to a remote location
B Coursebooks	designing criteria for selecting and evaluating coursebooks; identifying coursebook components
C Adapting and supplementing	adapting and supplementing a coursebook activity
D Technology and aids	assessing the current state of technological support
E Teaching without technology	suggesting ways of coping with minimal resources
Reflection	reflecting on key issues related to resources and technology

A Warm-up

1 This is designed to be a fun activity (and also a model of how to set up a 'pyramid discussion': the trainees first make their choices individually, then in pairs, then in groups of four and finally – if time allows – as the whole class, each time reaching a consensus within their group). It may be necessary to explain some of the items, e.g. Cuisenaire rods (variously coloured wooden rods of different lengths, originally used in the teaching of maths, but also associated with the Silent Way in language teaching).

2 Invite the pairs/groups to report their choices: in the discussion that ensues, some of the following points could be made: A coursebook may be of not much use if the level of the learners is not known; the mixed set of readers may be more exploitable. Likewise, the varied and topical input provided by the newspaper could provide useful content, especially if reinforced by dictionary use (in groups) and occasional grammar exercises. The visual aids might act as useful stimuli for talking as well as a source for vocabulary teaching. The digital recorder could be used for recording students, especially during structured conversation activities of the type associated with Community Language Learning. Teachers' resource books provide ideas that help vary the menu of activity types and a guitar could be used to accompany songs, thus providing some light relief. The Cuisenaire rods and the phonemic

chart are generally used to highlight features of form, but there are other means of doing this, so they are probably dispensable (the learner's dictionaries will have a list of phonemic symbols in them, for example). The encyclopedia may be of some use as a source of texts; the Shakespeare will be of interest only to certain high level learners.

B Coursebooks

1 Questions might include:
- Is the syllabus comprehensive, e.g. does it include grammar, vocabulary, functional language, etc.?
- Does the syllabus follow a logical and graded progression?
- Is there a good balance of activities, skills work, etc.?
- Is there sufficient variety, e.g. of topics, text types?
- Is the content interesting, topical, relevant?
- Are the texts authentic – or authentic-like?
- Are the texts well exploited, e.g. for both skills and language work?
- Is there sufficient language-focused work, e.g. grammar and vocabulary?
- Are the explanations clear and accurate?
- Do the activities follow a logical sequence?
- Is the material clearly laid out, well-illustrated and attractively designed?
- Is there a reference section?
- Are the teacher's notes clear and helpful?

2 Allow time for trainees, working in pairs or small groups, to evaluate their current coursebook and to report to the class on it. Perhaps use this discussion to point out why coursebooks are like they are, e.g. competitive global market, used in a wide variety of contexts, expensive to produce therefore unlikely to take risks, etc.

3 1–e) 2–a) 3–h) 4–c) 5–g) 6–i) 7–b) 8–f) 9–d)

4 The question of what is essential and what is optional is an open one and will depend on such factors as the learners' needs as well as the teacher's own teaching style. It's worth pointing out that it's unlikely that all this material could be used in the space of a normal (100-hour) course.

C Adapting and supplementing

1 Possible answers
a one-to-one: Working in groups would not be possible, but the teacher could do activity 9 too and the teacher and learner could take turns to do activity 10.
b an on-line, distance class: The group discussion can be conducted by means of a discussion board (students post messages to each other), or real-time chat.
c academic writing learners: Learners interview several other classmates, then write up a 'report' of their discussion, as if it were market research, for example.

2 Possible supplementary material might include: songs/stories/poems about childhood; extracts from novels, biographies, or autobiographies, in which people are reminiscing about childhood; or (extracts from) articles on the theme of child psychology. The materials could be used for skills development, reading/listening for pleasure; and as a springboard to further writing and/or speaking activities. Alternatively, material that has a high proportion of examples of *used to* could be found, e.g. concordance lines, and this material could be used for further study and reinforcement of the target structure.

D Technology and aids

1 Use the example to explain what a mind map is (if trainees don't already know). Organise the class into groups and assign a topic to each group. If possible, distribute blank overhead transparencies and pens, with which they can draw – and later present – their mind maps. Even if trainees are not familiar with the different technologies, they should be able to come up with some ideas of how they could be usefully exploited, but you may need to circulate, prompting with ideas of your own. Possible ideas include:

  a DVD/video player: playing extracts of film, TV, for listening comprehension, stimulus for speaking and writing, or background to extensive reading; playing extracts with the sound off, for brainstorming and/or scripting, before replaying with the sound on; lip-synching; pausing to elicit predictions as to what happens next; covering screen so that only subtitles are visible, to predict what is happening and then showing the full picture.

  b video camera: film learners performing a roleplay they have scripted and rehearsed; or a 'TV' panel discussion; learners themselves make a film based on a theme, or a series of 'vox pop' interviews; project work, e.g. on local cultural information, to exchange with students in another country.

  c OHP/data projector: use for grammar and vocabulary presentations; for projecting pictures to teach vocabulary; for projecting student work; for projecting texts, one line at a time, for predicting what comes next; for rapid viewing of pictures or text – *how much can you remember?*; for use by learners to give presentations to the class, e.g. 'show and tell', or (for business students) practice at giving business presentations.

2 a This is possible with video-conferencing, synchronous online chat programs and 'MOOs' – systems that allow multiple users to interact online in a virtual environment.

  b This is possible using corpora (databases of text), accessed online or on disks.

  c This is possible, to a certain extent, using voice-recognition software and interactive computer programs that model real conversation.

  d This is possible, to a certain extent, using programs that check spelling, grammar and stylistic features of texts.

  e This is possible using DVDs.

  f This is possible using hypertext links in a digital text that take the user to a dictionary, either online or on disk.

  g This is possible, to a certain extent, with voice-recognition software and programs that monitor accuracy of pronunciation.

  h This is possible using email, synchronous and asynchronous chat programs and bulletin boards, as part of a virtual learning environment (VLE), for example.

  i As (a).

  j This is possible using interactive whiteboards.

  k This is possible using software that assesses text difficulty, e.g. on the basis of word frequency, sentence length, etc.

  l This is possible, to a certain extent, using electronic translation programs.

  m This is possible using podcasting, for example.

3 In language classrooms, interactive whiteboards are useful for: displaying web-based resources to the whole class (e.g. texts, pictures); showing video clips; presenting, sharing and re-drafting students' work; manipulating text; and saving boardwork.

As an optional follow-up and as a means of getting the trainees to consider the arguments for and against IWBs (or any other technological innovation), they could perform this roleplay: in pairs, they take the role of a representative of a IWB manufacturer and a teacher. The former is trying to persuade the teacher to start using IWBs; the latter is sceptical.

E Teaching without technology

1 a Grammar presentation can be done by, e.g. using actions, mime, board drawings (as in the Direct Method), examples from the learners' own lives, etc.
   b Grammar practice, especially personalisation, does not require much in the way of aids: e.g. learners write true/false sentences incorporating the new structure. The teacher can also write gapped or jumbled sentences on the board; or can dictate sentences to transform, e.g. from active to passive.
   c Listening activities can be mediated by the teacher, either reading aloud/dictating texts, or telling the class stories, or acting out dialogues.
   d Texts can be written onto the board (e.g. in advance of the lesson) or onto posters; students can be encouraged to bring their own texts to the classroom, which they can write questions for and exchange with other students.
   e Testing can be done by dictating texts, sentences or questions, or by writing the test on to the board. Oral testing can take the form of interviews, roleplays, or individual presentations.
2 Ashton-Warner's concern to prioritise conversation and communication is consistent with the view (shared by many teachers and learners) that language learning should be communicative. It is also in line with the humanist position, whereby learners should be given maximum responsibility for their own learning.

REFLECTION

Allow the trainees to discuss the questions in pairs or small groups and conduct feedback in open class. Remind trainees that the contexts for teaching English vary enormously and that they may not be free to make decisions about the use (or not) of coursebooks, for example. They should be sensitive to the local conditions, including the expectations of their learners and the institutional constraints.

27 Introduction to language analysis

Main focus

An introduction to some core principles and processes in the analysis of language for teaching purposes.

Learning outcomes

- Trainees understand how language can be analysed from the perspective of text, of grammar, of vocabulary and of pronunciation.
- Trainees are aware that language analysis involves identifying parts of speech and the functional elements of a sentence.
- Trainees understand the importance of analysing language items in advance of teaching them, and know where to look for guidance in order to do this.

Key concepts

- meaning, concept; grammatical form
- context, function, style
- spoken and written form
- parts of speech
- sentence/clause elements; verb phrase
- similarities and differences between languages
- grammar references

Stage	Focus
A Warm-up	introducing key concepts through a matching task
B Multiple perspectives	learning to analyse language samples from different perspectives
C Parts of speech	developing the capacity to categorise words according to their class
D Sentence elements	learning the basic structure of sentences and applying this in a parsing task
E Contrastive analysis	comparing and contrasting some syntactic features of three languages with English
Reflection	using coursebooks as sources of guidance for language analysis

A Warm-up

1–e) 2–a) 3–g) 4–j) 5–b) 6–i) 7–d) 8–c) 9–f) 10–h).

B   Multiple perspectives

1   • warning = 5) function
   • stress = 7) pronunciation
   • use of modal verbs and passive voice = 2) grammar
   • words = 1) vocabulary
   • an airport = 8) context

2 a a set of instructions of the recipe type
   b It is found on the outer wrapping of a teabag, hence it would be found anywhere that tea is prepared.
   c to instruct
   d semi-formal, but with some features of advertising text, such as the positive-sounding words *perfect, freshly drawn, gently*
   e sets of words relating to topic: words relating to tea and tea-making (*cup, tea, bag, water, milk, sugar*); words with positive associations (see previous point)
   f distinctive features of its grammar: imperatives (*use, add, leave*); ellipsis (i.e. words that are omitted as in *Leave [it] standing; [It] Can be served*; *-ing* words (also called *participles*, i.e. *boiling, standing, stirring*) to describe actions extended in time; absence of an article (called *zero article*) before the uncountable nouns *water, milk, sugar.*

Note: Trainees should not be expected to identify all these grammar points correctly, but it may be worth pointing them out so as to demonstrate the potential of even short texts to embed a significant amount of grammar.

C   Parts of speech

Note: It may be a good idea to do the first two or three examples with the whole class, before asking the trainees to continue in pairs or small groups.

a

It	is	a	wonderful	life
pronoun	verb	determiner	adjective	noun

b

Gentlemen	prefer	blondes
noun	verb	noun

c

It	happened	one	night
pronoun	verb	determiner	noun

d

A	funny	thing	happened	on	the	way	to	the	forum
det.	adj.	noun	verb	prep.	det.	noun	prep.	det.	noun

e

The	postman	always	rings	twice
determiner	noun	adverb	verb	adverb

f

I	married	a	monster	from	outer	space
pronoun	verb	det.	noun	prep.	adj.	noun

g

And	God	created	woman
conjunction	noun	verb	noun

h

Stop!	or	my	mom	will	shoot
verb	conjunction	determiner*	noun	verb	verb

* Words like *my*, *your*, *her* are also categorised as possessive adjectives.

D Sentence elements

Note: As in the previous section, it may be a good idea to do the first two or three examples with the whole class, before asking the trainees to continue in pairs or small groups.

Subject	Verb	Object	Adverbial	Complement
a It	happened		one night	
b Mr Smith	goes		to Washington	
c Lady	sings	the Blues		
d The Empire	strikes back*			
e I	was			a teenage werewolf
f The Russians	are coming			
g Who	framed	Roger Rabbit		
h	Meet	me	in St Louis	
i I	promised	you (indirect object) a rose garden (direct object)	never (goes before the verb)	

* *Strikes back* is what is called a *phrasal verb,* consisting of a verb + particle. It would also be possible to analyse *strikes back* as VERB + ADVERBIAL.

In summarising this task, it is worth noting that *all* sentences have verbs and *most* have subjects. (The exception is h), where the verb is in the imperative form.) You could also point out that some verbs, like *prefer* and *frame*, take objects (they are called *transitive verbs*), while others, like *happen* and *come*, do not (they are called *intransitive verbs*). Some verbs, like *give*, *promise*, *write* and *buy*, take two objects: an indirect object and a direct object, respectively: *Give the dog a bone.*

E Contrastive analysis

1 and 2 You can adapt this task to the specific needs of the trainees by incorporating examples from the language(s) of the students they are teaching. For a useful source of information on language differences, see *Learner English* (2nd edition), edited by Michael Swan and Bernard Smith (CUP, 2001). On the evidence of the example sentences, the following syntactic features of the three languages should be noted:

Turkish: Turkish uses a subject–object–verb (SOV) word order; there is no independent verb *to be:* instead suffixes are attached to the relevant adjective or noun; the equivalent of English prepositions and possessive adjectives go after the noun; there is no definite article. Of these differences, the different article systems in Turkish and English cause the most problems. Turkish learners adapt quickly to SVO word order and prepositions.

Arabic: There is no present tense form of the verb *to be;* there is no indefinite article; there is no exact equivalent to the English genitive construction (*rich man's houses*); adjectives follow the noun; in the equivalent of relative clauses, an object is obligatory (*This is a letter which a famous lady sent it*). All of these differences (apart from adjective order) are transferred into English (causing *L1 interference*, or *negative transfer*).

Japanese: Like Turkish, Japanese is an SOV language; Japanese employs a number of markers (or particles) to indicate, for example, the topic, subject and object of the sentence; the equivalent of English prepositions go after the noun; subject pronouns are usually omitted: *Ate an apple.* There are no articles as such in Japanese, and plurality often goes unmarked (*zoo* = elephant/elephants). These last two differences probably cause more problems than any of the others.

REFLECTION

In reviewing this task it may be helpful to show trainees examples of reference books and websites that are useful for analysing language for teaching purposes. (See the Further Reading list in the *Resource File* for examples.)

28 Tense and aspect

Main focus

To analyse verb forms in terms of tense and aspect, with special reference to the present, and to identify ways of teaching these forms.

Learning outcomes

- Trainees understand the difference between (grammatical) tense and aspect.
- Trainees can distinguish between the form and meaning of the present simple, present continuous and present perfect.
- Trainees can apply this analysis to identifying the objective of coursebook activities, and to designing a presentation.

Key concepts

- tense: present, past
- aspect: continuous, perfect
- present simple/continuous/perfect

Stage	Focus
A Warm-up quiz	reviewing the trainees' knowledge of verb phrase grammar
B Verb forms	using a text to identify and contextualise present and past verb forms
C Basic concepts	distinguishing the concepts that underlie the principal verb forms
D Learner problems	analysing examples of typical learner errors
E Materials	identifying the focus of specific teaching materials
F Classroom application	applying the above analysis to the presentation of verb forms
Reflection	a short review

A Warm-up

1 The quiz can be set as a pre-session task. Since trainees are also invited to review it at the end of the session ('Reflection'), you may decide to delay checking the answers until they have reached that stage.

Quiz answers

1 Technically, there are only *two* grammatical tenses in English: the present and the past. This is because English verbs are inflected only for present and past, e.g. *goes, went*. The future is formed by using auxiliaries (*will go, going to go*). All other so-called 'tenses', such as present continuous, past perfect, future perfect continuous, are really combinations of tense and aspect. For practical purposes, however, these are referred to as tenses. (See the *Brief guide to the English Verb* on page 201 in the Trainee Book.)

2 auxiliary 3 participle 4 *done*: it is the only one which is a past participle 5 *yesterday*: the present continuous doesn't normally have past reference (although it can be used, like the past

continuous, in telling narratives in the present tense) 6 *last year*: the present perfect is not normally compatible with a specific time reference.

B Verb forms

1 Depending on the nature of their pre-course task, some trainees may already be familiar with the names of the basic verb forms. For those who aren't, it would be a good idea to provide reference books to help with this task, e.g. a standard students' grammar, such as *English Grammar in Use*, by Raymond Murphy (CUP).

   a *runs*: present simple; *told*: past simple; *was training*: past continuous; *'d become*: past perfect; *isn't working*: present continuous; *'ve taken*: present perfect.

   b Other examples are: present simple: *(don't) want, enjoy*, as well as the present tense forms of the verb *to be*: *she's …, it's …, I'm … there's …*; past simple: *didn't think, said, knew, wanted, did*, as well as the past tense forms of the verb *to be*: *it was, I was*; past continuous: *was happening*; past perfect: *I'd (always) liked*; present continuous: *I'm getting*; present perfect: *That's worked, I've achieved*. (Note that *he's got* takes the *form* of the present perfect, but has present simple meaning.)

2 The completed table should look like this. (Other examples from the text are also possible.)

Tense	Aspect	Examples
present	(no aspect = simple)	*Jo Thornley runs her own plumbing business*
	continuous	*now I'm getting older*
	perfect	*I've taken on an apprentice*
past	(no aspect = simple)	*I told my friends*
	continuous	*I was training as a plumber*
	perfect	*I'd become very unhappy*

At this stage, it may be worth making the following points:

- The apparent complexity of the English verb system is misleading: all structures (apart from those that are not marked for aspect) are simply combinations of the two tenses with the two aspects.
- Future forms do not figure in the above table, as these are dealt with under modality – which is the 'third element' in the equation.

C Basic concepts

1 *runs* vs *ran*: the latter implies completion and distance, i.e. no connection with the present.
2 *was* vs *am*: the latter denotes 'present-ness', vs completion and distance.
3 *runs* vs *running*: by emphasising the ongoing and unfolding (i.e. progressive) nature of the activity, the latter implies lack of permanence, or temporariness.
4 *isn't working* vs *doesn't work*: again, the former implies 'at the moment' vs a more durable 'fact'.

5 *achieve* vs *have achieved*: the latter connects the present to the past, and refers to achievements that took place in a period from the past to the present, while the former refers to achievements in general at any time (past, present, future).

6 *have taken* vs *took*: the latter is remote and distant, unconnected to the present (the apprentice may have left), while the former implies some present relevance, e.g. recency, and/or present evidence (the apprentice is still here).

7 *trained* vs *was training*: the former construes the training in its entirety while the latter, emphasising its unfolding nature, implies that it was a process, which may or may not have been completed.

8 *had become* vs *became*: the former situates the event prior to another past point of reference, while the latter *is* the past point of reference.

2. 1–d); 2–c); 3–f); 4–b); 5–a); 6–e)
You should point out that the concepts in the right-hand column are the most common concepts associated with these structures. But they are not the only ones. Any one structure can express a (limited) number of *different* concepts, depending on such things as the context and the choice of verb. Thus, the present continuous can also express future arrangements (see below) and the past perfect can also be used to express hypothetical past events, as in *If someone <u>had known</u>* …. Trainees should be advised to 'do their homework' when teaching these verb forms, and consult reliable reference sources.

D Learner problems

Point out that some of these errors are simply 'mis-formations', i.e. the learners has used the wrong form of the right structure, while others are 'mis-selections', i.e. the wrong choice of structure, while still others may be a combination of both.

a *not enjoying*: mis-formation: the verb in the continuous takes the *-ing* form.

b *are you eating*: mis-formation: the auxiliary in the continuous is the verb *to be*.

c *went*: mis-selection: use the past simple to talk about past events.

d *didn't pass*: mis-formation: use the base form of the verb in negative constructions in the past.

e *did you do*: mis-selection: use the past simple to talk about events situated in a definite time in the past, hence unconnected to present.

f *was walking*: mis-selection: use the continuous form to talk about an ongoing activity that "frames" a past event.

g *had already started*: mis-selection: use the past perfect to situate the event prior to a previously established past reference point.

E Materials

The first exercise targets the use of the negative auxiliary (form) and deals with the 'general truth' use of the present simple (meaning). The second activity focuses on the present continuous, and in particular its use to refer to temporary situations in the present (meaning). The third activity focuses on the present perfect and in particular the meaning associated with duration from the past to the present.

F Classroom application

Organise the trainees into groups, and assign one structure per group. They should devise a situational presentation for their structure, and preferably one that generates several examples of the same structure. Monitor the preparation stage, and check that the trainees have identified the correct form for the item in question. Once the task is completed, either re-group the trainees so that they can explain their ideas to other trainees, or, alternatively, ask individuals to demonstrate their presentation to the whole class. (This may require allowing time for the preparation of simple visual aids.)

REFLECTION

These two activities can be set as homework.

29 Meaning, form and use: the past

Main focus

To distinguish between a focus on form, on meaning and on use, in the analysis and presentation of grammar items, with special reference to past tense verb forms.

Learning outcomes

- Trainees understand how grammar items can be analysed in terms of their form, meaning and use.
- Trainees can apply this distinction to the analysis of past tense verb structures, and can use this analysis to inform a presentation of these structures.
- Trainees understand the importance of identifying and anticipating problems that learners have with meaning, form and use.

Key concepts

- the past: past simple, past continuous, past perfect
- contexts of use: narrative
- timelines
- typical problems: meaning, form, use

Stage	Focus
A Warm-up	taking part in, and observing, a past narrative
B Past verb forms	focusing on the form, including written and spoken, of the three different past tense forms
C Focus on meaning	using contrasted pairs of sentences to focus on the meaning of the different past tense forms
D Focus on use	using a short text to focus on the way that past tense forms are used in narrative
E Learners' problems	identifying and analysing learners' errors
F Classroom application	applying the analysis of past tense forms to a presentation task
Reflection	identifying the meaning, form and use focus in published materials

A Warm-up

Trainees work in groups of three. Two members in each group will have a conversation, while the third listens and notes details. If there is time, they can then swap roles – one of the speakers becoming the observer. Give each observer a copy of the observer's task (below). You may decide to limit the number of items that each observer listens for, but between them they should cover all five items.

Conduct a general class feedback on the observer's task, writing some of the examples on to the board. If they noted down time expressions or linking expressions, see if they can recall the verbs that were associated with them. If you have examples of the past simple, past continuous and past perfect, write these up and identify them. You could also invite individuals to tell the whole class any of the more interesting stories that came up, and, again, these may provide useful sources for examples of the target structures.

OBSERVER'S TASK

Listen to the conversation, and note down any examples that you hear of the following:

a time expressions, e.g. *a few years ago, last month*
b any expressions of the type *I was doing X when* …
c any expressions beginning *I'd (never/just …)* or *I hadn't* …
d any questions with *did, was, were,* or with the verb *happen.*
e any linking expressions, such as *then, after that, finally.*

© Cambridge University Press 2007

B Past verb forms

Trainees can work in pairs on these activities; each activity should be checked before they continue to the next.

1 1–c) 2–d) 3–a) 4–f) 5–e) 6–b)
2 Rule 3 refers to the spoken form (i.e. the pronunciation) and rule 2 to the written form (i.e. the spelling).
3 Point out to trainees that the term *progressive* is often used instead of *continuous.*

Rules about the formation of the past continuous	Examples
1 The past continuous is formed with *was* or *were* plus *-ing* (the present participle).	*It was raining. They were watching.*
2 The negative is formed by adding *not (n't)* to the auxiliary verb.	*It wasn't raining. They weren't watching.*
3 Questions are formed by inverting the subject and the auxiliary verb, followed by the *-ing* form.	*Was it raining? What were they doing?*
4 Negative questions are formed by adding *not (n't)* to the auxiliary verb.	*Wasn't it raining? What weren't they doing?*

4

Rules about the formation of the past perfect	Examples
1 The past perfect is formed by the past of the auxiliary verb *have* plus the past participle.	*It had rained. Someone had taken it. The train had left.*
2 The negative is formed by adding *not (n't)* to the auxiliary verb.	*It hadn't rained. The train hadn't left.*
3 Questions are formed by inverting the subject and the auxiliary verb, followed by the past participle.	*Had it rained? Why hadn't the train left?*

In concluding this section, it is important to emphasise that all the above rules are rules of *form*. They provide no information about the *meaning* or *use* of these forms.

C Focus on meaning

1 The timelines could be completed like this:

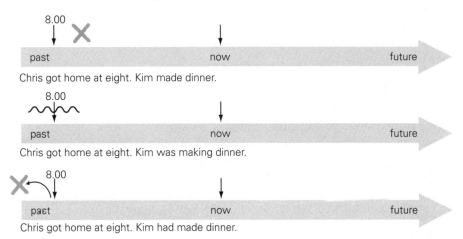

Chris got home at eight. Kim made dinner.

Chris got home at eight. Kim was making dinner.

Chris got home at eight. Kim had made dinner.

2 If trainees are having difficulty forming rules, prompt them by asking questions such as:
- Which form is used to refer to one-off events that are viewed as being complete? (*past simple*)
- Which form emphasises the event's continuity or duration? (*past continuous*)
- Which form views the event from the perspective of a viewpoint in the past? (*past perfect*)

Some simple rules based on the examples are:

past simple: to refer to past situations, usually disconnected from the present

past continuous: to refer to situations in progress in the past; these may be unfinished, interrupted, or repeated

past perfect: (when we are already talking about the past) to refer to an earlier past time (or *anterior* time).

D Focus on use

Establish that *use* refers to the way that a language item functions in context. An analogy could be made with a car: you can describe what a car looks like, how its parts work and that it is designed to move from A to B. But this does not explain the multiple uses that a car is put to – such as taking the children to school, or car racing, or even as a temporary home. An item's *use* can be fully appreciated only when it is observed in its typical contexts, hence the choice of an extract of authentic narrative text for this task.

Point out that the tenses are used to situate the events in time, and in relation to one another, so that it is possible to flash forward and back, or to frame events 'inside' others. You could ask the trainees to recall any instances of tense shift in the anecdotes that they told in the warm-up activity.

a past simple: *said, slowed, slowed, took, looked, lowered, had:* past continuous: *were driving, was driving, was running, was slowing down;* past perfect: *'d spent.* There are also a number of examples of the past form of the verb *to be,* describing past states: *was (still scorched), were (about sixty miles south …)* and *could,* the past of the modal verb *can,* to describe past ability.

b past simple

c past continuous

d past perfect

E Learners' problems

1 and 2 Write these sentences on the board.
- I bought it yesterday.
- I buyed it yesterday.
- I have bought it yesterday.
- I have buyed it yesterday.

Use these examples to demonstrate the distinction between (1) the correct choice of tense in its correct form, (2) the correct choice of tense in an incorrect form; (3) incorrect tense in correct form; and (4) incorrect tense in incorrect form.

a *fighted* = correct tense, wrong form (should be *fought*)

b *was going* = well-formed, but wrong choice of tense (should be *went* or *used to go*)

c *heared* = correct tense, wrong form (should be *heard*); *don't stopped* = correct tense, wrong form (should be *didn't stop*)

d *weared* = wrong form (should be *wore*) and wrong tense (should be *was wearing*)

e *didn't arrive* = well-formed, but wrong choice of tense (should be *hadn't arrived*)

f *spended* = correct tense, wrong form (should be *spent*)

g *rangs* = correct tense, wrong form (should be *rang*)

h *didn't be* = correct tense, wrong form (should be *wasn't*)

i *go* = well-formed, but wrong choice of tense (should be *had gone*)

j *didn't have arrived* = correct tense, wrong form (should be *hadn't arrived*)

3 The problems that learners have are primarily:
- not knowing the correct form of the past tense, especially for irregular verbs, with a tendency to overgeneralise the *-ed* ending, e.g. *fighted, weared*.
- misapplication of the auxiliary for marking negation, as in *didn't stopped, didn't have arrived*
- failure to select the correct tense to mark anterior time (past perfect), or to distinguish between events seen as a whole (past simple) and events seen as unfolding over time (past progressive)

F Classroom application

1 Organise the class into groups of three or four and assign a structure to each group. Remind them of the basic principles underlying an effective grammar presentation (see Classroom Teaching Units 6 and 7). It is not necessary to script a detailed lesson plan; simply that they should agree on a way of presenting the meaning (e.g. using a situation or scenario) which is representative of the way that the structure is used. They should show that they know at what stage – and how – to present and highlight the form.

2 Re-group the trainees so that they can exchange their ideas. One way of doing this is to assign each member of each group a number (1, 2, 3, etc.), and then ask all the number 1s to sit together and all the number 2s to do likewise, etc.

REFLECTION

For this task the trainees could use the coursebook that they are currently using with their teaching practice class. Alternatively, assign different groups different coursebooks representing a range of levels. Allow time for trainees to comment on – and ask questions about – the way the books deal with this area of grammar.

30 Expressing future meaning

Main focus

To analyse the main ways of expressing future time and to identify ways of teaching them.

Learning outcomes

- Trainees understand the main ways that future meaning is expressed in English.
- Trainees can distinguish between the form and meaning of *will*, *going to* and the present continuous.
- Trainees can apply this analysis to identifying the objective of coursebook activities and to designing a presentation.

Key concepts

- *will*, *going to*, present continuous, present simple
- future continuous, future perfect
- predictions, intentions, arrangement
- time clauses
- contrastive presentation

Stage	Focus
A Warm-up	trainees perform a language practice exercise in order to generate data for analysis
B Future forms	using a grammar explanation to identify different future forms
C Learner problems	identifying, correcting and explaining learner errors with future forms
D Grammar presentation (1)	analysing a coursebook presentation of a future form (*will*)
E Grammar presentation (2)	analysing a contrastive presentation of two future forms (present continuous and *going to*)
F Classroom application	applying the above analysis to the preparation of a contrastive presentation (*will* vs *going to*)
Reflection	a review quiz

There is one optional activity that supports the unit.

The optional activity requires learners to exploit an authentic text for the purposes of focusing on ways of expressing the future.

A Warm-up

1 Set up this activity exactly as you would with a class of learners. Avoid indicating what structures they should use. Allow trainees time to compare their answers in pairs or small groups and to briefly discuss them, although at this stage the discussion should be about the content, not the form.
2 If trainees are unlikely to be familiar with the names of the different future forms, you could skip activity 2 and move directly to B.

B Future forms

1 Trainees should perform this task in small groups, pooling the sentences they generated in the warm-up stage and matching them to the descriptions in the *Language Reference*. Note that in the *Language Reference*, the wording is ambiguous: the slash between *predictions/decisions* … should be interpreted as a semicolon (;).

2 There may be some debate as to whether the explanations account for all the examples that the trainees produce: you may need to point out that *futurity* is an area that is difficult to pin down – not least because it is largely conjectural. (Swan (2005) notes: 'This is a complicated area of grammar: the differences between the meanings and uses of the different structures are not easy to analyse and describe easily. In many, but not all situations, two or more structures are possible with similar meanings' (p. 186).) The trainees, like learners, may have to settle for 'rules of thumb'.

You may also wish to highlight that *going to* is followed by an infinitive and trainees can use this to distinguish it from the present continuous.

Note also that Unit 31, which deals with modality, is also relevant to the topic of futurity.

3 The conventional order for introducing these structures is:
   Beginners/elementary:
   * present continuous (arrangements): ease of form and concept. (The form is likely to have been already covered when referring to the present.)
   * *going to* (predictions and intentions): usefulness, frequency and relative ease
   * *will* (offers, etc.): usefulness
   Intermediate:
   * *will* (predictions): usefulness and frequency. (Note that, contrary to received wisdom, *will* is the most common way of expressing futurity, both in speech and writing.)
   * *if/when* …: usefulness, clauses
   * *might/may*: usefulness, frequency and ease
   Upper-intermediate/Advanced:
   * future continuous and future perfect: relatively infrequent structures

C Learner problems

1 Point out that correcting learners' errors in expressing futurity is not always simple, since it assumes an understanding of what their intended meanings were. The following corrections are based on the most likely intended meanings. (Incidental errors of vocabulary, etc., have not been corrected.)
   a The moment I get home today I am going to play a computer game. Then I am going to eat a sandwich.
   b Once this lesson has finished I'm going to meet my friend [or I'm meeting my friend] because we're going to go to the cinema [or we're going to the cinema]. After maybe we'll take (we'll have) a coffee in any café.
   c Once this lesson has finished I'll go to my house. I'll read the newspaper and prepare a nice dinner. I'm not going to watch TV.
   d When I have enough money … I will never have enough money! But if I do/did, I will (or would) visit many countries.
   e When I'm next on holiday I'll spend/'m going to spend a good time with my family.

   f This time next year I will be studying for my final examination. I don't think my life will be much different.

   g In five years' time may be I'll have a better job. I'd like to start my own business.

   h By the time I retire I hope I will have saved enough money for buy a nice house by Black Sea.

2 Explanations are:

   a Auxiliary verb required, omission of subject and verb not possible.

   b Indicator of future intention/plan is needed (*going to* or present continuous), as well as (non-planned) prediction (*will*).

   c *Going to* might be more normal for all these instances, especially in spoken language and it is definitely preferred in the negative, as *won't* implies refusal rather than simply negative intention.

   d Adverb comes between auxiliary and main verb. In a subordinate clause beginning *if*, the future form is not necessary. The 'hypotheticalness' of the statement suggests that a (second) conditional form might be more appropriate.

   e Present continuous in its future use is used only with arrangements, rather than intentions or predictions. (Note also that *have a good time*, or *spend time*, are the more usual collocates.)

   f Future continuous more probable here, since the 'studying' will be in progress. *I don't think* + affirmative is the more usual way of making a negative prediction (rather than *I think* + negative).

   g *Going to* expresses an intention or a prediction that is based on present evidence, but the use of *maybe* implies a prediction that is more like a hope. *I'd like …* is a form of conditional statement.

   h The context suggests that the 'saving' will start before the 'retiring'.

3 The pronunciation problems stem from the use of contractions or weak forms, where the tendency of learners is to pronounce the auxiliary verbs in their uncontracted and/or strong forms (*What will you do …?*) with a consequent negative effect on the rhythm. *Won't* is often pronounced *want* by learners, which can lead to confusion: **The children want go to bed.*

D Grammar presentation (1)

Sections D and E could be done by two different groups working simultaneously; the trainees can then be re-grouped in order to report their findings to trainees from the other group.

1 a *will/won't*

   b prediction

   c a situation, from which a number of sentences have been generated

   d questions about the underlying notion and about the form (in the box labelled 'Grammar').

2 Possible practice activities include:

  • asking learners to make more predictions based on the situation

  • providing a different (future) situation

  • asking learners to make predictions about it.

E Grammar presentation (2)

1. a present continuous and *going to*
   b arrangements/plans vs predictions
   c a text, with several examples of each of the target structures in context
2. A possible follow-up activity would be a gap-fill text, where the choice between the present continuous and *going to* is determined by the context.

F Classroom application

1. Point out that the two structures *will* and *going to* are often contrasted, but usually only in their *intentional* (or *volitional*) sense, where they are used quite differently: *I'll have the chicken/I'm going to have the chicken.* (Compare this to their *predictive* sense, where they are often interchangeable: *I think it will rain/I think it's going to rain.*)

   Trainees should refer to the previous section for ideas as to how to design a grammar contrast based on a text. Suggest that they include more than one example of each of the two structures in their text. The material in section D shows ways of checking learners' understanding of both form and meaning.

   If time allows, ask volunteers to demonstrate their presentation to the class. (They may need to make copies of the text they plan to use.)

Note that, if the trainees are teaching a group of the appropriate level, the presentation could be targeted at this particular group – and even used with that group.

REFLECTION

Quiz answers
1. not in any strict sense, since there is no single form of the verb that expresses the future
2. *will*, *going to*, present continuous
3. *will*, *going to*
4. present simple
5. a yes
   b not necessarily: assessment of certainty is usually expressed by a modal verb (*may, might*) or by adverbials (*perhaps, definitely*)
   c yes
   d no
   e yes, this can sometimes determine the choice between *going to* and *will*, for example – the former being more characteristic of informal, spoken language than formal written.

Optional activity: Using an authentic text

Select an authentic text which contains several examples of future forms. Ask trainees how they would exploit the text (thinking of pre-, during- and post-reading/listening tasks). They should then consider what aspects of grammar they would focus on and how they would present these to a class, before also thinking about possible follow-up practice activities. You will need to tell them the level of class they should consider, and different groups could consider different levels.

31 Modality

Stage	Focus
A Warm-up	trainees are introduced to the core formal and semantic properties of modal verbs
B Modal verbs in context	using a text to identify and describe some common modal verbs
C Modal verbs: form	identifying the formal features of modal verbs
D Modal verbs: meaning and use	identifying the kinds of meaning expressed by modal verbs, their typical functions, and contexts of use
E Classroom application	making syllabus decisions about modal verbs; identifying the aims of coursebook materials and writing a dialogue to contextualise modal verbs
Reflection	reviewing issues of form and meaning using an error correction task

A Warm-up

1 There are three verbs in sentence a), four in sentence b) and two in sentence c).
2 The lexical verbs are: a) *swimming* b) *swimming* c) *swim*.
3 *Have* and *been* are auxiliary verbs providing tense and aspect meaning (see Unit 28), i.e. they have a grammatical function.
4 Sentence a states a fact and sentence b expresses the speaker's belief about, or attitude to, the fact.
5 The modal verb is *must*.
6 A situation where this sentence would be appropriate would be one where the speaker wasn't a hundred per cent sure that some people had been swimming, but where there was good evidence to suggest as much, e.g. wet hair.

7 The modal verb is *may*.

8 The two meanings can be paraphrased as: i) She will probably swim. and ii) She is allowed to swim.

Point out that the dual-meaning nature of *may* is shared by all modal verbs. Note that it is not important at this stage to go into the meanings of other modal verbs. It is important, though, that the trainees write down (either individually or collaboratively) some questions they want answered and that they return to these in the final reflection stage.

B Modal verbs in context

1 The modal verbs in the text are: *will, must, should, can, be able to, have to, may, would*. Note that we are using the term 'modal verb' here to include both the 'pure modals' (*can, must*, etc.) and what are sometimes called marginal modals, semi-modals or (as here) modal phrases (*have to, be able to*).

2 1 *have to, be able to*

   2 Pure modals are those that take the form of auxiliary verbs, unlike *have to* and *be able to* (compare the questions: *Must I?* and *Do I have to?*). The other pure modals are *could, shall* and *might*. *Need* and *ought (to)* are also included in this list, although they do not fulfil all the formal criteria of pure modal verbs.

   3 Point out that these are the meanings that these verbs express in *this* context, but that they are not the only meanings they can express (as will be shown below).
   necessity: *must, have to*; probability: *will, can (be physically demanding), would*; ability: *can (speak fluent Arabic), be able to*; desirability: *should*; permission: *may*.

   4 You don't have to have previous experience.

C Modal verbs: form

1 Point out that, in speech, the modals have weak forms, a fact which causes learners problems of perception: 'We /kən/ work it out'.
   1–e) 2–d) 3–a) 4–c) 5–b)

2 1–c) 2–e) 3–a) 4–f) 5–b) 6–d)

D Modal verbs: meaning and use

1 Explain that modals are often associated with particular language *functions* because they express a range of meanings that have to do with the way people interrelate.
   a i) possibility/probability; ii) permission
   b i) prohibition; ii) (negative) possibility/probability
   c i) possibility/probability; ii) willingness (also called *volition*)
   d i) obligation; ii) possibility/probability
   e i) ability; ii) possibility/probability
   f i) (negative) possibility/probability; ii) (negative) volition

2 Possible answers
   a *May I sit down? Can we leave our bags here?*
   b *You should/ought to/had better (lie down.)*
   c *Can/could/will/would you (open the window?)*
   d *I'll (do the dishes) Shall I (clear the table?)*

e *I'll (pay you back.)*
f *I'll/I shall (phone the police.)*
g *Would (you like a drink?)*

3 Possible answers

a asking permission: in a museum, e.g. asking permission to take photographs.

b giving advice: friendly advice to someone who is ill, worried; 'problem page'; giving a tourist advice; careers adviser

c asking someone to do something: workplace; obtaining a service, e.g. at the drycleaner's, hairdresser's, etc.

d offering to do something: as a guest in someone's home; helping someone who is lost, overburdened, etc.

e promising: as return for a favour, e.g. in the home, workplace; student to teacher

f stating an intention: ordering a meal, booking a hotel, flight, etc.

g inviting: restaurant, hotel, home.

E Classroom application

1 The materials deal with the following areas:

Text	Modal verb	Meaning	Type
A	*will*	making offers, a function of volition	practice exercise
B	*could have done, should(n't) have done, needn't have done*	possibility in the past, (un) desirability in the past, (lack of) necessity in the past	practice exercise
C	*can, allowed to, have to, mustn't*	permission, obligation, prohibition	presentation

2 Organise the trainees into pairs or groups of three and assign each group one of the structures. Establish the level at which the structure is likely to be taught (by reference to the syllabusing task above). Alternatively, choose structures that are relevant to the level of students that trainees are teaching, or that are included in their current coursebook. Remind trainees of the kinds of contexts in which the structures typically occur.
Point out that dialogues should aim to be *representative* of the item's use, rather than highly imaginative, funny, etc. – although, of course, an element of originality may make the dialogue more memorable.

3 Check that the dialogues do provide a clear and exploitable context for the targeted items. If time allows, invite individuals from each group to demonstrate how they would use their dialogue in class.

REFLECTION

1 a Can you help me a minute?
   b What time do you have to start work?
   c I must go now. Bye-bye.
   d We are not allowed to wear jeans at school.
   e We can't do what we want.
   f I don't have to do the washing and ironing because my mother does it for me.
   g You can't smoke in here. It's against the rules.
   h My mother has to work very hard six days a week.

2 All the errors, apart from (f) are errors in the formal features of modal verbs; (f) is an example of the wrong choice of modal verb, which has an effect on meaning.
   a Auxiliary *do* is not required in questions.
   b Auxiliary *do* is required in the question. (*Have* is a lexical verb, not an auxiliary.)
   c *To* is not required with the infinitive.
   d *Be allowed to* follows the grammar of the verb *to be*.
   e Negative should be formed by adding *n't*.
   f Negative obligation should be expressed by *don't have to*, not *mustn't* (which is used to express prohibition).
   g Infinitive should follow modal.
   h *Have to* obeys rules of lexical verbs, so needs third person singular form.

3 Allow the trainees time to discuss any residual problems relating to modality. If time does not allow a full discussion of these, trainees can be referred to a teacher's grammar, e.g. *Grammar for English Language Teachers*, by Parrott (CUP).

32 Conditionals and hypothetical meaning

Main focus

To learn the main patterns and meanings of conditional sentences.

Learning outcomes

- Trainees understand the main formal characteristics of conditional sentences and can identify the different meanings and functions associated with them.
- Trainees know of other ways of expressing hypothetical meaning.
- Trainees can apply this knowledge to the design of a presentation.

Key concepts

- conditional clause, conjunction
- hypothetical meaning; real vs unreal conditions
- first, second, third and mixed conditionals
- functions of conditionals: warning, giving advice, etc.

Stage	Focus
A Warm-up	matching sentence halves of conditional sentences
B Conditional sentences	studying rules and finding examples
C Related forms	comparing conditional patterns with other ways of expressing hypothetical meaning
D Learner problems	identifying and correcting errors
E Functions and contexts	identifying possible functions and contexts for conditional sentences and designing a presentation
F Coursebooks	evaluating the treatment of conditionals in coursebooks
Reflection	reflecting on issues related to the analysis of conditional forms

A Warm-up

1 Trainees work in pairs to complete the matching task. An alternative approach might be to copy and cut up the sentence halves and distribute them. Trainees memorise them and then mill, repeating their fragment until they have found their 'other half'.

1–g) (Prince); 2–e) (Barbra Streisand); 3–j) (Martina McBride); 4–f) (Simply Red); 5–b) (Elvis Presley); 6–a) (Reba McEntire); 7–c) (Luther Ingram), 8–i) (Cher); 9–d) (Elvis Presley); 10–h) (from the musical *Mame*).

Ask the trainees if they can think of any other lines of songs with *if* in them (such as *If I had a hammer* ...) and add these to the 'corpus'.

2 Those that express unreal conditions are: 1–g), 3–j), 5–b), 6–a), 8–i) and 10–h).

B Conditional sentences

1 1 Types 2 and 3 express unreal conditions.

2 The significant form feature is the 'backshift' in tense in the conditional clause (beginning with *if*), where the past tense is used for present or future meaning; and the past perfect is used for past meaning. A similar backshift takes place in the modal verb of the main clause (*will* → *would*; *can* → *could*, etc.; and *would do* → *would have done*).

2 a Type 1: 2–e), 4–f); Type 2: 1–g), 3–j), 5–b), 8–i) and10–h); Type 3: 6–a).

b Examples 7–c) and 9–d) don't fit any of the types.

c They have the pattern *if* + present + present; this pattern is called the 'zero conditional'.

C Related forms

1 This relates to the second conditional; both use past forms to refer to present/future situations.

2 These link to the third conditional; both grammatical patterns use the past perfect and refer to past situations.

Regarding the question of differences in form, there is only a subordinate clause for *If only …* and *I wish …* (with the main clause implied), whereas typical conditional forms require a main clause. Regarding differences in use, *If only* and *I wish* express regret, rather than the wide range of meanings associated with a corresponding conditional pattern.

D Learner problems

a Despite having future reference, the future form should not be used in the *if* clause.

b Over-generalisation of type 2 (unreal) conditionals to a real situation. (This was allegedly said by a Swiss orchestra conductor to a restless audience, meaning *If you don't like it, you can go!*)

c Mixing past forms (*could*, for unreal conditions) with future form (*will*, for real conditions); i.e. confusing type 2 and type 1.

d Transposing the verb forms in the two clauses.

e Failure to use past tense after *wish* to express unreal (hypothetical) present meaning.

f Failure to use past perfect to express unreal (hypothetical) past meaning.

E Functions and contexts

1 If trainees have not yet covered Unit 33 *Language functions*, you will need to explain that a function is the communicative *purpose* for which an utterance, or sequence of utterances, is used. Note, too, that, in the absence of more information as to the speaker and their purpose, the functions and contexts in this task are speculative. However, the task demonstrates some of the more typical uses for conditional sentences.

Model sentence	Type	Likely function	Possible context
If you're not careful, you'll cut yourself.	1	warning	parent to child who is playing with scissors
I would've called you if I'd known you were ill.	3	regretting, apologising	friend to friend after an absence
If I were you, I'd join a gym.	2	giving advice	friend to friend, or doctor to overweight patient
If you like romance, you'll love this film.	1	recommending	film critic in a review
I'd live in the town centre if I could afford it.	2	imagining, hypothesising	friend to friend, discussing housing
If you need anything, just help yourself.	0	offering	parents to babysitter; friend to guest
If you'd been here on time, we wouldn't have missed the flight.	3	blaming	couple at airport check-in

2 Organise the class into groups for this task, and assign each group a model structure. Remind them of the different ways of conveying the meaning of a structure, eg, through a situation, a text, a dialogue or personalisation. Point out that the *form* of conditional sentences is particularly problematic and therefore deserves special attention. Also, point out that the concentration of contractions and weak forms in conditional sentences can cause fluency problems for learners, and may need to be targeted for special treatment, such as drilling. If time allows, ask individuals from each group to give their presentation to the class.

F Coursebooks

Most coursebooks (except at very low levels) will have something on conditional patterns. At higher levels they may include mixed conditionals. Although most coursebooks follow the sort of analysis given in this unit, it is possible that some will analyse conditional patterns differently. You may wish to supply alternative coursebooks for the trainees to consider in order to broaden their experience of published material.

REFLECTION

a The real/unreal distinction has the advantage of being simpler, and of explaining most mixed conditionals as well as the zero conditional. It also allows for past real conditions (as well as present ones), such as *When we were young we spent our holidays at the beach. If it was sunny, we would spend all day on the beach, but if it rained we'd go to the local cinema.* The traditional three-way distinction does not allow for this (admittedly infrequent) kind of meaning. However, the three-type distinction is the one still favoured by most coursebooks.

b As examples of mixed (or anomalous) conditionals, you could write up the following (also song lyrics):
If there hadn't been you where would I be? (Billy Dean)
If you fall in love tonight you're gonna be alright. (Rod Stewart)
If you're thinking you want a stranger, there's one coming home. (George Strait)
Should I fall behind, wait for me. (Bruce Springsteen)
Ask the trainees to invent combinations of their own, and to test each other, to see if they sound plausible.

c All conditional constructions, except the zero conditional, use modal verbs in their main clause.

33 Language functions

Main focus

To describe language in terms of its communicative functions and to apply a functional approach to teaching.

Learning outcomes

- Trainees understand how utterances have a communicative function and that there is no one-to-one match between utterance and function.
- Trainees understand how context factors affect the interpretation of an utterance, as well as the choice of an appropriate style.
- Trainees learn how a functional approach has informed syllabus design and they can apply these principles to the design of teaching materials.

Key concepts

- form vs function
- context and register
- appropriacy
- functional exponents; functional syllabus

Stage	Focus
A Warm-up	matching utterances to contexts
B Context and function	assigning functions to utterances and relating the idea of function to context factors
C Function, style and language	introducing the notion of appropriacy and the inclusion of functional exponents in syllabus design
D Classroom application	trainees write dialogues that contextualise and contrast functional exponents
Reflection	trainees reflect on the role of appropriacy in language learning

A Warm-up

These activities are designed to introduce the idea that language and context are interrelated and that a key factor of the context is the interpersonal relationship between speakers. Activity 2 simply draws attention to the linguistic features of utterances, while the rest of the session is concerned with pragmatics – the ways that utterances are interpreted in the light of their contexts.

1 1–c) 2–a) 3–f) 4–e) 5–b) 6–d)
2 b   imperative (*tell*); infinitive (*to be*)
   c   present of *to be* (*is*); infinitive (*to get*)
   d   present continuous
   e   imperative (*turn*); present continuous; infinitive
   f   past simple

3 Explain to trainees that each caption represents what is being said by one of the speakers in the cartoon. Something that somebody says is called an *utterance*.

  a context: at 'front door'; relationship: acquaintances (social equals)

  b context: work, restaurant; relationship: restaurant manager to waiter (familiar, but difference in social rank)

  c context: doctor's surgery; relationship: doctor–patient (probably familiar, but difference in social rank)

  d context: library; relationship: librarian–library user (probably not familiar and difference in social rank)

  e context: home; relationship: mother and child (familiar, but difference in age)

  f context: school; relationship: teacher and pupil (familiar, but difference in social rank and age)

B Context and function

You could begin this section by writing up some signs such as NO SMOKING and MIND THE GAP – or by drawing attention to existing signs in the classroom. Establish the communicative function of these signs. Point out that the function may be explicit in the language, for example SMOKING IS PROHIBITED, but in the sign THANK YOU FOR NOT SMOKING the function appears to be 'thanking', but in fact it is probably also 'prohibition'. In other words, its intended function is not explicit and has to be inferred.

1 a apologising

  b commanding

  c giving advice

  d warning

  e making a request

  f making an excuse

Point out that functions are usually expressed as *-ing* forms. This underscores the fact that they describe how speech acts are *performed*. It also distinguishes them from *notions*, which are more abstract concepts such as *duration, frequency, quantity*, etc.

2 The utterances where the function is explicit are:

  a <u>Sorry</u> we're late, we had trouble finding you. = marker of apology

  b Well, my <u>advice</u> to you is to get a less powerful sports car. = noun describing type of speech act

  c <u>Tell</u> Luigi to be a little more careful with the pepper. = imperative

  e <u>Please</u> <u>turn</u> it down. = request marker and imperative

3 To identify the function of the non-explicit (indirect) utterances, context factors such as the *place* (e.g. a library, a school) and the *relationship* (e.g. librarian (adult)–library user (child); teacher (adult)–pupil (child)), need to be considered.

4 a telling the time (asking for information)

  b expressing impatience

  c teaching

  d complaining

5 Possible contexts and functions are:
   a someone being bothered (threatening); someone at the scene of a crime (offering)
   b someone in a cold room (stating a fact); couple watching TV (requesting)
   c couple watching TV (requesting); hotel porter showing guest their room (stating a fact)
   d tired driver to passenger (requesting); car rental clerk to client (asking for information)

C Function, style and language

Explain to trainees that just as an utterance like *I'll call the police* can perform different functions according to its context, so too can one function, such as *warning*, be realised in different ways. Show that it is possible to warn someone about something by saying any one of the following:

Be careful doing that.
I wouldn't do that, if I were you.
If you do that, X might happen.
Do that and X might happen ...

Explain that the choice between one of several different ways of performing a language function depends on a number of *context* factors. These factors will include such things as whether the message is spoken or written, the relationship between the people involved (such as how well they know each other) or the social distance between them.

1 Possible utterances/texts might be:
   a We're having a few friends around tomorrow evening and we were wondering if you'd like to come over for a 'welcome drink'.
   b Fancy a drink?
   c Will you be wanting your umbrella today? (and/or) Do you mind if I take it/your umbrella?
   d Hello, X. This is Y here. I wonder if you could do me a big favour? I won't be able to pick Z up from playschool today. Do you think you could possibly pick her up and drop her home?
   e Might I suggest the library provide a DVD lending service?
   f How about/Have you thought of lowering your computer?

In the discussion that might ensue when checking this activity, point out that the way context factors influence language choices is not a feature of English alone, but is a universal characteristic of language. The main problem that learners will have is not knowing exactly how social distance is encoded in English (compared to, say, languages like French, which has a *tu–vous* distinction). In English, social distance is often signalled by the use of past tense forms, conditional constructions and modal verbs.

2 1–d) 2–b) 3–c), f) 4–a), e).
3 Note that most coursebooks now include functional descriptors in their contents, but these may not always be labelled as such, or they might be interspersed in the grammar, thematic, or skills strands of the course, sometimes as *Everyday English* or *English in situations*, etc.

D Classroom application

Organise the trainees into groups of three to five. Give each group a function to work on. For example:

- asking permission
- making a request
- complaining
- apologising and making an excuse
- greeting

Remind trainees that they need to think of *two* different situations, where the difference is in the degree of formality. The context should be a recognisable one and easy to set up. For the demonstration, suggest that the 'teacher' use his or her colleagues to perform the dialogues as if they were an audio or video recorder. In discussing the presentations, ask for suggestions as to how these could be developed into practice tasks.

REFLECTION

Points that should emerge from this discussion are:

a An exclusive focus on language forms may mean that learners are ill-equipped for a lot of day-to-day language functions, especially those that involve interpersonal relations (such as requests, asking permission, etc.) where expressing degrees of politeness and formality may be crucial.

b Teaching only language functions may reduce the course to a succession of phrasebook-type utterances, from which it may be difficult to generalise the grammar.

c Make sure the distinction between *accuracy* and *appropriacy* is clear – the former being formal correctness, the latter being the way an utterance matches its context, especially the relationship between speakers. Most second language learners will be able to recall times when they used the wrong register (e.g. in the choice of *tu* or *vous* forms), or when an intended meaning – such as asking for information – was interpreted differently – e.g. as a request or a complaint.

34 The noun phrase

> **Main focus**
>
> To analyse noun phrase formation in English, in relation to problems learners have and ways of addressing these problems.
>
> **Learning outcomes**
> - Trainees can identify and analyse different noun phrase (NP) formations in English.
> - Trainees can analyse and correct learner errors in this area.
> - Trainees can identify the objective of teaching materials that target aspects of NP form and use.
>
> **Key concepts**
> - noun: countable vs uncountable nouns
> - pronoun: personal, possessive
> - adjective
> - noun phrase: pre-, post-modification, head
> - determiner: definite and indefinite article; quantifier
> - relative clause

Stage	Focus
A Warm-up	experiencing a game that focuses on an aspect of NP formation
B Noun types	identifying and analysing NPs in a text
C Learners' problems	analysing and correcting NP errors
D Classroom application	identifying the objective of different coursebook activities with a NP focus
Reflection	analysing a written text and comparing it to a spoken one

A Warm-up

1 Explain the game as follows:
One person starts and says *I went to market and I bought* [an item]. The person to their immediate left repeats this and adds an item of his or her own. The game continues, each person repeating all the previous items and adding a new one. For the purposes of this session, the items should fit the pattern *a/an X of Y*, as in *a kilo of tomatoes, a jar of olives, a loaf of bread*, etc.
Start the game off yourself and then delegate a trainee to follow. The game can be played as a whole class, or, if the group is very large, in smaller groups seated in circles.

2 In discussing the game, it should be noted that any activity that provides opportunities for both creativity and repetition is good for language learning, since it optimises memorability. Also, the fact that the game involves the repetition of *lexical chunks* is consistent with the view that a lot of language use involves the retrieval and production of memorised multi-word items.

3 The game can be adapted for other noun phrase forms by, for example, using the rubric *I went on holiday with* [*my brother's wife*, etc.] or *I went to a party and I met* [*the Queen of England*, etc.].

B Noun types

1 The aim of this activity is to identify all the different grammar elements that, alone or in combination, make up noun phrases. It may help to start this activity off in open class, before allowing the trainees to continue it in pairs or groups of three. It may also help to make dictionaries available. Remind trainees that they don't have to find *all* the examples of the different items, but only one of each – or, in the case of determiners, four. Examples of the different items include:

  a singular nouns: *chapter, teacher, organiser, controller, detail, class, nature, language,* etc.
  b plural nouns: *roles, languages, skills, concerns, teachers, aids.*
  c countable nouns: all the above plural nouns, as well as *chapter, teacher, class, lesson, classroom,* etc.
  d uncountable nouns: *detail* (in this context), *nature, language* (in *the nature of language* and *grade their own language*), *management, chaos.*
  e pronouns: *we, it, they.*
  f adjectives that pre-modify nouns: *previous, various, basic, important, own, biggest, new, common, technological.* (Note that there are some adjectives in the text that do not pre-modify nouns, such as the first instance of *important* and *appropriate.*)
  g nouns that pre-modify other nouns: *classroom, management.*
  h post-modifying clauses: *that a teacher is called upon to fulfil,* [*that*] *a teacher needs to develop,* [*that*] *they are teaching.*
  i determiners: *the, a, this* [*chapter*], *these, some, every, any, one of, their, most* [*new teachers*].

2 The first extract illustrates how many nouns in English can be used both in a countable sense (*how languages may be learned*) or in an uncountable sense (*the nature of language*). Other more concrete examples include *glass, coffee, hair, paper, chicken,* etc. The second extract illustrates the distinction between indefiniteness and definiteness, as signalled by the use of *articles. A class* is indefinite (no known class is being referred to); *the class* is definite since it is defined by the relative clause that follows (*they are teaching*) or because it refers to the whole group of items of which this is a member (*controlling the class = controlling classes*). Another, more concrete, example is: *A tiger roared. I heard the same tiger roar again. The tiger hunts by night.* Point out that issues of countability and definiteness are crucial in choosing the correct determiners to go with nouns. The indefinite article *a/an,* for example, cannot be used with uncountable nouns: **a chaos.*

3 Make sure that trainees understand that a noun phrase (NP) is one or more words which has a noun (or pronoun) as its main part. Ask trainees to consider which element all the NPs have in common and to notice what often goes before and after this element. The examples all have in common a phrase *head,* i.e. the noun that expresses the main concept. This head may be pre- and/or post-modified. For example:

pre-modification	head	post-modification
the previous	chapter	
a	teacher	
the	nature	of language
Ø basic classroom management	skills	
Ø	chaos	
the	class	they are teaching
one of the biggest	concerns	for most new teachers
Ø common technological	aids	

Explain that pre-modification typically involves the use of determiners, adjectives and other nouns; and that post-modification typically involves the use of *of*-constructions, prepositional phrases (*for most new teachers*) and relative clauses. Note also that the symbol Ø represents the *zero article*, i.e., the absence of an article before uncountable nouns, or plural countable nouns that are used with an indefinite sense.

Point out also that pronouns (such as *we*) can form a noun phrase. Pronouns are not normally pre-modified, but can be post-modified as in *Anyone who knows the answer put your hand up*.

C Learners' problems

1 This task can be done using a teacher or student grammar reference book. Assign specific errors to different groups; they can then re-group to explain their errors to each other.
   a Failure to use plural form (*friends*).
   b Adjectives precede nouns.
   c Uncountable nouns do not have a plural form.
   d Uncountable nouns take a zero article.
   e Noun modifier is preferred (*train timetable*).
   f Noun modifier is usually singular (*bus station*).
   g Possessive *'s* is usually used only when the first noun is a person; instead use an *of*-construction: *the floor of the room*.
   h *Any* (meaning unrestricted quantity) is more usual in questions.
   i Zero article is used when talking about a class of things.
   j *Most of* + NP is used with the definite article *the*; for indefinite articles use *most* + NP; *a few* is used with countable nouns; for uncountable nouns use *a little*.
   k The relative pronoun for people is *who*.
2 The correction strategies that the trainees choose may include the following; they are all aimed at prompting self-correction:
   • verbal prompts, e.g. *plural?*
   • echoing and querying: *I am the student which…?*
   • gesture, so as to reverse the word order (e.g., b; e, g)
   • brief explanation, e.g. '*Information*' is uncountable.
   • concept checking question, e.g. *Has she got one hair, or a lot of hair?*
   • clarifying and reformulating: *Do you mean the 'bus station'?*

D Classroom application

1 The activities target the following areas:

A post-modification, using participle clauses and prepositional phrases

B articles, specifically the use of the zero article to make general statements

C choice of determiners with countable and uncountable nouns, specifically, *much, many, some, any*

D different kinds of determiner that express quantity (*quantifiers*)

2 Activities A and C are typical presentations, using a context (a dialogue in both cases).

3 They could be followed by some kind of controlled exercise, e.g. a gap fill, or creating more sentences using prompts (such as pictures); and/or personalisation.

REFLECTION

1 and 2 The noun phrases in the text can be analysed like this. Note that some noun phrases are embedded in others.

Pre-modification	Head	Post-modification
your	language	
the	level	of the learners you are teaching
the	learners	you are teaching
a very important teaching	skill	
the	models	you give learners
Ø	learners	
the	language	which it is appropriate to use with a low level class
a low level	class	
the	language	used with a higher class
a higher	class	
every	word	you say

3 In the spoken text the noun phrases are much less lengthy and complex than in the written one; there is more use of personal pronouns (*you*); there is also a higher proportion of verbs to nouns in the spoken text.

The use of complex noun phrases is a distinguishing feature of much factual writing (such as technical and academic writing, journalism, etc.) and it is therefore a skill that many learners need to acquire. Simply learning the grammar of spoken language (including its reliance on verbs) may not be sufficient preparation. Point out that the majority of errors that learners make in writing are NP errors.

35 The sounds of English

Main focus
To learn how English sounds are classified, described and represented.

Learning outcomes
- Trainees understand the difference between (spoken) sounds and (written) letters.
- Trainees are able to read and write phonemic transcription of consonant and vowel sounds.
- Trainees are aware of how sounds are simplified in the stream of speech.

Key concepts
- phoneme: vowel, diphthong, consonant
- phonemic script: the phonemic chart
- sounds in connected speech: simplification
- minimal pairs
- contrastive analysis

Stage	Focus
A Warm-up	experiencing an activity focusing on sound discrimination
B Sounds vs letters	focusing on the difference between letters (graphemes) and sounds (phonemes)
C Consonant sounds	introducing and practising the way consonant sounds are represented
D Vowel sounds	introducing and practising the way vowel sounds are represented
E Sounds in connected speech	focusing on the way sounds are affected by their environments
F The phonemic chart	introducing the phonemic chart and activities associated with its use
Reflection	a quiz of some of the main content of the session

A Warm-up

1 Write the following names on cards, or photocopy and cut up the table. Distribute the cards so that each trainee has one. If there are more than 20 trainees, you may have to invent more names, e.g. *Joan Bird*, *Jean Bird*, etc. Tell the trainees that these are their 'new names', that they should memorise them and keep them secret. Then 'call the class register', i.e. call out names randomly. When the trainees hear their 'name', they answer 'Present'. In the event that more than one trainee answers to the name, call it out again until the problem is resolved.

Jan Bird	Jan Baird	Jan Burt	Jan Beard
Jon Bird	Jon Baird	Jon Burt	Jon Beard
Jen Bird	Jen Baird	Jen Burt	Jen Beard
Jim Bird	Jim Baird	Jim Burt	Jim Beard
Jem Bird	Jem Baird	Jem Burt	Jem Beard

© Cambridge University Press 2007

2　1　Learners are more likely to fail to discriminate between many of these names, since they may not share the same sound differences in their first language.

　　2　The language targets the phonological system of English (as opposed to the grammar or vocabulary systems, for example) and, specifically, the pronunciation of individual sounds, especially vowels.

B　Sounds vs letters

1　Dictate the following words: *letter, sound, vowel, consonant, phoneme*.

2　Note that *phoneme* is the technical term for a sound and specifically one that makes a difference in meaning, such as the *-ir-* sound in *bird* and the *-ear-* sound in *beard*.

3

Word	Number of letters	Number of sounds
letter	six	four
sound	five	four
vowel	five	four
consonant	nine	nine
phoneme	seven	five

Point out that, depending on your regional accent, you may not pronounce the word identically to other speakers. For example, a speaker of AmE [American English] might pronounce the final *r* of *letter*, making five sounds in all.

4　Establish the fact that there is no one-to-one match between letters and sounds. In focusing on pronunciation, it is important to distinguish between the way words are written and the way they are actually pronounced.

C　Consonant sounds

1　Make sure that trainees know that consonant sounds are formed when the airflow from the lungs is obstructed by the movable parts of the mouth, including the tongue and lips. At this stage of their training it is probably unnecessary for trainees to know the terminology for describing the manner and place of consonant production (such as *bilabial plosive, palato-alveolar fricative*, etc.), since this terminology is rarely if ever used in teaching materials. It is sufficient to know that consonant sounds are produced at various points in the mouth, from the lips to the soft palate – and beyond.

2 a) met b) deck c) then d) hedge e) breath f) fetch g) next h) yet i) shred j) shrink

3 Point out that the vowels are written either /e/ (as in *ten*) or /ɪ/ (as in *tin*). Note that it is customary to write phonemic symbols within slashes: /freʃ/.
   a) /sent/ b) /edʒ/ c) /θɪn/ d) /θɪŋ/ e) /θɪŋk/ f) /ðɪs/ g) /fɪkst/ h) /dʒest/
   i) /jeld/ (or /yeld/ using American transcription) j) /stretʃt/

D Vowel sounds

Again, no attempt has been made to describe vowel sounds in terms of tongue position or lip rounding. Note that the American system of transcription is less standardised than the British one. We have adopted the system used in Celce-Murcia, Brinton and Goodwin, *Teaching Pronunciation*, Cambridge University Press, 1996. You may also wish to point out that the five British English vowel sounds followed by the sign ː, i.e. /iː/, /uː/, /ɔː/, /uː/ and /ɜː/ are known as *long vowels*, in contrast to the *short vowel* sounds, which are not so marked.

1 a) Batman b) King Kong c) Airplane d) Jaws e) The Birds f) Psycho g) Young
    Frankenstein h) Chicago i) Doctor Zhivago j) Jaws 2.

2 British English a)/ʃrek/ b) /ben hɜː/ c) /snætʃ/ d) /staːwɔːz/ e) /haɪ nuːn/ f) /bleɪd rʌnə/
   g) /məmentəʊ/ h) /mɪstɪk rɪvə/
   American English a) /ʃrek/ b) /ben hɜ^r/ c) /snætʃ/ d) /star wɔrz/ e) /hay nuwn/
   f) /bleyd rʌnə^r/ g) /məmentow/ h) /mɪstɪk rɪvə^r/

3 Check the trainees' transcriptions, especially where they are likely to be negatively influenced by the spelling of a word. Check, also, that the *schwa* sound is being used correctly.

E Sounds in connected speech

This section aims to raise trainees' awareness as to the existence of such features of connected speech as *assimilation*, *elision* and *linking*, but it is not important that trainees know these terms.

1 The following effects are likely to occur:
   a The /t/ will be dropped at the end of *last* (= elision).
   b The /t/ will become more like a /k/ because of proximity to /g/ (= assimilation).
   c There is a change in the quality of /t/ at the end of *great*, so that it tends to merge with the /d/ of *dictator* (= assimilation).
   d The /n/ merges with the /m/ (= assimilation).
   e The /d/ is dropped and /n/ merges with /b/ (= elision and assimilation), so that it sounds like 'Stam by your...'
   f A /r/ is introduced between *war* and *of* (= linking).
   g A /j/ is introduced between *we* and *are* (= linking), so that it sounds like 'weyare'.

2 The implication for learners has more to do with *reception* than production: they will often not recognise words in spoken language because of these context effects.

F The phonemic chart

At this stage you might like to introduce a discussion about the benefits – for both teachers and learners – of knowing how to read and/or write phonemic script. It is worth noting that all learners' dictionaries now use this script and a number of coursebooks will also incorporate it. But more important, perhaps, is simply knowing how many sounds there are in English and being able to compare the sound system of English with that of the learners.

1 a **Lesson A:** This is a correction technique. **Lesson B:** This is a way of teaching the pronunciation of new vocabulary. **Lesson C:** This is a 'minimal pairs' teaching technique, where two closely related (and hence possibly confusable) sounds are contrasted in word contexts that differ in only this respect.

   b **Lesson A:** This technique assumes that learners already know what the symbols stand for. **Lesson B:** Again, this assumes prior knowledge of the symbols. **Lesson C:** This technique does not assume any special knowledge of phonemic script, although the use of symbols avoids confusion with spelling conventions, especially with vowels, where one sound may be spelled in many different ways. Note that the warm-up activity that began this session is a kind of minimal pairs activity.

2 Speakers from different language groups will have different problems with English phonemic contrasts. The /p/ vs /b/ distinction is a problem for Arabic speakers, for example. /l/ vs /r/ is (famously) a problem for speakers of Japanese, Korean and Chinese. Most learners will have problems distinguishing the full range of English vowel sounds. (See *Learner English*, by Swan and Smith (CUP, 1987, 2001) for a full treatment of cross-linguistic differences.)

REFLECTION

This activity could be set as a kind of race, with trainees competing in small groups to be the first to produce all the correct answers.

a 26

b In RP: 44 (24 consonants + 20 vowels). In NAE: 40(24+16).

c Consonants are produced by interrupting or obstructing the airflow; for vowels, the airflow is simply modified, but not interrupted.

d /s/ is voiceless; /z/ is voiced.

e *Schwa*

f /ɪ/ is a monophthong, while /aɪ/ is a diphthong.

g /z/

h /ɜː/ (or /ɜʳ/ using the North American system)

i True (Shakespeare wrote *Macbeth*.)

j False (New York is *not* in Texas.)

36 Stress, rhythm and intonation

Main focus

To learn how suprasegmental features of pronunciation (such as stress, rhythm and intonation) influence meaning and intelligibility.

Learning outcomes

- Trainees understand the basic mechanics of stress, rhythm and intonation.
- Trainees understand how stress, rhythm and intonation influence meaning.
- Trainees understand how these principles can be incorporated into the design of classroom materials and activities.

Key concepts

- word stress, syllable
- sentence stress
- new vs given information
- strong and weak forms
- rhythm, stress time vs syllable time
- intonation, pitch
- grammatical, attitudinal functions of intonation
- high vs low involvement

Stage	Focus
A Warm-up	experiencing communication using only intonation
B Stress	working out some regularities in word stress assignment and learning how sentence stress distinguishes between given and new information
C Rhythm	learning how low-information words are accommodated into the rhythm of an utterance, including the distinction between strong and weak forms
D Intonation	distinguishing between the grammatical and attitudinal functions of intonation
Reflection	discussing the relative importance and ease of teaching segmental and suprasegmental features

A Warm-up

1 In setting up this activity, it may help to write the following on the board:

A: well	B: well
A: well	B: well
A: well	B: well

Challenge trainees to imagine a conversation consisting of this single word. Then ask them to read the instructions in their book.

151

This activity demonstrates how much meaning can be conveyed by means of intonation alone. It is worth pointing out, though, that the kinds of meaning that are conveyed are fairly limited and that they are also reinforced by facial expression, gesture and voice quality.

2 Most learners would have little trouble doing this activity, assuming they understood the words of the dialogue and that they were relatively uninhibited. Attitudinal features of intonation – such as expressing uncertainty or surprise – are probably universal.

B Stress

1 The activity demonstrates that word stress in English, while not 100% regular, is generally fairly predictable. However, proficient speakers are able to assign stress correctly not because they know the rules (which are complex), but because of their previous encounters with similar words. Some general tendencies that can be extracted from these examples are:
- In two-syllable words the stress tends to be on the first syllable, especially where the second syllable is a suffix (**paw**ler, **ved**dish, **mal**mer).
- Polysyllabic words tend to be stressed on the antepenultimate syllable, i.e., the third-to-last: **pan**diful, **loo**mitive, **im**belist.
- However, certain suffixes, such as -ic, -tion, 'attract' the stress: loo**mi**tion, imbe**lis**tic.
- This accounts for stress shift in word families: **ge**on, ge**on**ics, etc.

You could ask trainees to think of real word examples for these different tendencies.

2 Techniques for highlighting word stress include:
- providing a clear, even exaggerated, model
- asking learners 'Where's the stress?'
- 'finger-coding', i.e. using the fingers of one hand to represent the syllable structure of the word and drawing attention to the stressed syllable
- drilling the word
- tapping out the stress pattern, humming it, or using any other non-linguistic way to show the pattern, such as using different coloured Cuisenaire rods
- writing the word on the board with an indicator of prominence, e.g. a small box, above the stressed syllable
- grouping words with the same stress pattern together

3 1 The sentence stress shifts according to the speaker's assessment of what the listener needs to focus on. Sentence stress (unlike word stress) is variable.

2 As a general rule, *new* information – as opposed to *given* information – is stressed. Note that this is a particularly difficult skill for many learners to master, since – in many languages – sentence stress plays a less influential role in distinguishing new information than does word order, for example.

4 and 5 If trainees are in doubt as to the meaning of stress shift, use the previous task to demonstrate it. Alternatively, set up an exchange between yourself and a trainee of the type:
Where do you LIVE?
In X. Where do YOU live?

C Rhythm

1 Point out that this is another example of a classroom activity that trainees could do with their students. The object is to maintain the same rhythm while *accommodating* intervening syllables by reducing them in different ways.

1 The individual words are accommodated by the use of *contractions* (*should've*) and of *weak forms*, e.g. /ʃəd/ rather than /ʃʊd/.

2 The 'squeezing' and 'swallowing' of the low-information words can be a problem for students when listening, as these words are difficult to perceive. And failure to use weak forms and contractions can make their spoken language sound stilted, while failure to stress the high-information words can make their message difficult to unpack.

You could point out that English is sometimes classified as a *stress-timed* language, i.e. one where the stressed syllables occur at regular intervals, so that intervening syllables are accommodated to fit the rhythm. This contrasts with *syllable-timed* language (like Spanish or Chinese) where the syllables are given approximately the same length. (This distinction has been challenged by some theorists, who argue that stress timing only occurs under certain conditions and is not generally perceptible in normal speech.)

2 The activity focuses on the difference between *strong forms* and *weak forms*, a distinction that affects most of the common *function words* in English – such as auxiliary verbs, determiners, prepositions and conjunctions.

3 The use of weak forms is an important factor in achieving a native-like *rhythm* (see above).

D Intonation

Note that this section on intonation deliberately avoids a detailed discussion of the different pitch direction and pitch span distinctions that are often related to differences in grammatical meaning, since most trainees (and learners) find these difficult to perceive. Nor does it discuss the *discoursal function* of intonation, i.e. the role of intonation in the management of talk, since this is seldom if ever represented in teaching materials. For a more detailed analysis, see *English Phonetics and Phonology* (third edition), by Peter Roach (CUP, 2000).

1 Note: You can model the difference between these sentence pairs yourself.

The objective of this activity is to highlight the *grammatical* and *attitudinal* roles of intonation. The grammatical role includes the way that intonation serves to 'package' information by segmenting utterances into *tone groups*, as in the example about Chinese opera and in the utterances (a),(b) and (c):

a (1) the people who left suddenly | started running (= Some people left suddenly; they started running.)

 (2) the people who left | suddenly started running (= Some people left; they suddenly started running.)

b (1) my brother who lives in New York | has a penthouse (= defining relative clause)

 (2) my brother | who lives in New York | has a penthouse (= non-defining relative clause)

c (1) she didn't marry him | because of his parents (= His parents were the reason she didn't marry him.)

 (2) she didn't marry him because of his parents (= She married him for some other reason.)

Utterances (d) and (e) can be used to show how intonation helps distinguish between statements and questions, including question tags (e) – another grammatical function.

Utterance (f) is related, in that *Mexico City*, when uttered with a falling intonation shows *certainty*, whereas a rising one shows *uncertainty*, a case of grammatical and attitudinal meaning merging.

Utterance (g) can be used to show the distinction between *completion* (falling tone on the last word) or *incompletion* (rising tone), as in lists. It is the example that most closely represents the discoursal function of intonation.

Finally, examples (h) and (i) can be expressed in a variety of different ways to convey the speaker's attitude, ranging from *high involvement* (using a broad pitch span and high *key*) or *low involvement* (the opposite).

2 Intonation helps to package information and to make distinctions between statements and questions, certainty/uncertainty, completion/incompletion and high and low involvement.

3 Failure to use intonation in these ways can distort the speaker's message and lead to misunderstandings, as well as threatening interpersonal communication, such as when speakers seem to be conveying low involvement.

4 Activity 1 focuses on the attitudinal role of intonation and Activity 2 on the difference between 'real' questions and confirming questions, using question tags. Note that the exercises are based on transcripts of recordings, but that the trainees don't need to hear the recordings to be able to identify the purpose of the activity. As a follow-up, you could ask trainees to read the transcripts aloud in the way that they would probably have been recorded.

REFLECTION

Points to emerge from this discussion are:

a There is still some debate as to which features of pronunciation are critical in ensuring communication, a current view being that suprasegmental features, such as stress and rhythm, are more important than segmental features, such as the pronunciation of individual phonemes.

However, the issue is complicated by the fact that few if any features operate in isolation (so it is difficult to single out what exactly has caused a communication breakdown) and also the fact that such variables as the *listener's* proficiency, previous exposure and first language, also play a role. Given that many English users need English to interact, not with native speakers, but with other non-native speakers, the goals of pronunciation teaching are in the process of being re-defined.

Research suggests that – for successful communication between non-native speakers – features such as the pronunciation of individual vowel sounds and intonation are less critical than consonant sounds and the correct placement of sentence stress.

b 'Learnabilty' will be influenced by factors such as the learner's L1 and the amount of natural exposure they get, but most (adult) learners always have difficulty mastering the full range of English vowel sounds, using intonation in a native-like way, distinguishing between weak and strong forms and placing stress correctly in sentences. Perhaps the 'easiest' area is word stress, since learners steadily accumulate exemplars (rather than rules) through exposure and practice.

37 Teaching pronunciation

> **Main focus**
> To explore a variety of techniques and activities for teaching different features of pronunciation.
>
> **Learning outcomes**
> - Trainees review principles and issues of pronunciation teaching.
> - Trainees are aware of how these principles are realised in teaching activities.
> - Trainees know how to integrate pronunciation teaching into their classes.
>
> **Key concepts**
> - intelligibility; accent reduction
> - segregated vs integrated activities
> - segmentals/suprasegmentals
> - reception vs production
> - contextualised vs decontextualised
> - pre-emptive vs reactive teaching
> - RP/English as an International Language

Stage	Focus
A Warm-up	reviewing areas of pronunciation and main issues related to its teaching
B Pronunciation activities	identifying the objective of a range of activities and evaluating them
C Anticipating problems	identifying typical problems associated with some common language areas and designing a teaching strategy
D Classroom application	identifying areas of pronunciation teaching that could be integrated into activity sequences
Reflection	reviewing terminology and principles

A Warm-up

1 The areas are: a) word stress b) sounds (specifically vowels) c) intonation d) sentence stress e) sounds (consonants) f) rhythm.
2 The following points should be made:
   a RP is the standard model for pronunciation in coursebooks and dictionaries published in Britain, but its status has been challenged on the grounds that it does not represent the majority of English accents, and, more importantly, because for learners who are learning English as an International Language (EIL), it may be an inappropriate model. Nevertheless, in the absence of a viable alternative, it is likely to remain the dominant model. This does not necessarily mean, though, that teachers should adopt RP for teaching purposes.
   b That 'segmental' features (i.e. the pronunciation of individual sounds) are less critical than suprasegmental ones is the accepted wisdom, but the picture is probably more complicated than this simple distinction suggests. For example, while the pronunciation of individual vowel sounds makes little difference in terms of intelligibility, the *length* of the

vowels can have an effect. Also, the features seldom work in isolation, so it is not always easy to determine the exact cause of a misunderstanding.

c The view that you should teach a lot of pronunciation, and soon, has generally been discredited, as research has shown that pronunciation – like other aspects of language learning – tends to follow its own developmental route.

d The prioritising of intelligibility over accuracy is associated with the communicative approach; it is also more realistic, as there are some features of pronunciation (such as intonation and the pronunciation of individual sounds) that are resistant to instruction. And, given that few adult learners will achieve native-like pronunciation (or may even want to), 'comfortable intelligibility' may be a more appropriate goal.

e A natural and conversational speaking style on the part of the teacher (including the use of contractions and weak forms where appropriate) provides learners with useful listening practice as well as a good model for their own production. This does not mean that the teacher should be a native speaker, but simply that they should avoid adopting an artificial 'teacher's voice'.

B Pronunciation activities

1 To start this activity, it may be a good idea to do the first activity in open class, before organising the class into pairs or groups to continue.

a This is a receptive activity, focusing on a 'small' (i.e. segmental) and decontextualised feature of pronunciation. It is not communicative at all, since there is no interaction and nothing is being communicated. It would be difficult to make it more communicative since the feature in question has little effect on intelligibility.

b This is another receptive activity, and focuses on the relationship between sound and spelling; there is neither context nor communication. The activity could possibly be made more meaningful (if not more communicative) if the cards showed *pictures* of the items, rather than the words.

c This is a productive activity, and focuses on the use of sentence stress in correcting errors of fact (a 'big' – or suprasegmental – feature) in context. It is very communicative: it requires both listening and speaking and attention to meaning as well as to form.

d This is a productive activity focusing on the attitudinal use of intonation, and it is (minimally) contextualised and communicative.

e This is a productive activity, and the focus will vary according to the errors the students make; it is highly contextualised and communicative (although if the teacher corrects *all* errors, rather than only those that threaten intelligibility, it may cease to be communicative, and just become an exercise in 'getting it right').

f This is a productive activity and focuses on all features of pronunciation at once (hence it could be described as *holistic*), but especially targets the suprasegmental ones, such as rhythm and intonation; there is a context, but the activity is not communicative. It could be made more communicative if an extra stage were added, where learners were asked to incorporate some of the 'rehearsed' language into original conversations.

2 In evaluating these activities, trainees should be allowed to express their subjective opinions: some may like the game-type element of, say (b), while others may find the constant correction in (e) off-putting. Nevertheless, the issues of *context* and *communicativeness* (highlighted in the previous activity) offer criteria by which these activities can be judged more objectively. Also, activities that are *only* receptive may have limited usefulness in terms

of improving learners' pronunciation. Note that activity (e) (correcting during speaking activities) is an example of *reactive* (as opposed to *pre-emptive*) teaching, and some researchers argue that it is the more effective.

C Anticipating problems

Note: The language areas for this activity could also be selected from the syllabus of the trainees' current coursebook. You could ask different groups to start at a different item (*a*, *b*, *c*, etc.), to ensure that all items are covered, even if time is short.

1 Possible problems include:
   a *can/can't*: failure to discriminate between weak and strong forms, so that *can* sounds like *can't*; use of the same vowel sound for both *can* and *can't* plus failure to articulate final *t* in *can't*, so that, again, the two words sound the same.
   b ordinal numbers: the main problem is the /θ/ sound, at the end of regular ordinals (*fourth, tenth*, etc.), especially for learners whose first language does not include this sound. Also problematic might be *consonant clusters*, as when /θ/ follows another consonant, as in *eighth, twelfth*, although, in reality, even native speakers elide (i.e. drop) the first consonant of the cluster.
   c *used to*: tendency to pronounce /s/ as /z/; failure to use weak form of *to*; inserting an extra syllable: /juːsɪd/
   d present simple questions: rhythm, particularly the use of the weak forms of *do* and *does*. Assimilation also occurs with *do you*: /dʒuː/ and *don't you*: /dəʊntʃuː/.
   e *would you mind…-ing?*: intonation, which, if flat or falling, might not convey sufficient politeness; failure to elide *would you*; the /ŋ/ sound at the end of the present participle may cause problems for some learners.
   f clothing vocabulary: vowel phonemes, particularly the difference between /ɜː/ and /ɔː/, as in *shirts/shorts*, but also the wide range of other vowels and their different spellings (e.g. *suit, shoes*). Word stress may also cause problems in compound nouns, such as *overcoat, pullover, swim suit*.

2 Assign different pairs/groups one or two of the syllabus areas to work on. Possible solutions:
   a recognition: discriminating between *can* and *can't*, in isolation and in sentences; production: short dialogues with both *can* and *can't*.
   b recognition: minimal pairs exercises, e.g. contrast *thing/sing, moth/moss*, etc.; production: demonstration of the /θ/ sound (tongue between teeth), repetition in isolation and in words.
   c recognition: discriminating between *an axe is used to chop wood; he used to live next door;* etc.; production: drills; practice in sentences, dialogues, 'jazz chants', with emphasis on rhythm: *I used to be fat but now I'm thin …*.
   d recognition: Asking learners to identify main stress in sentences like *What do you do? Where do you live?*, etc.; boardwork to show main stresses; production: drills (to encourage natural rhythm and use of weak forms), 'shadowing' (see above).
   e recognition: contrasting 'low involvement' with 'high involvement' intonation; production: drills, dialogues, etc.; practice making requests for different situations, ranging from informal, friendly, to formal, distant.
   f recognition: minimal pairs exercises to focus on contrastive vowel sounds; categorizing words according to stress; production: sentences with high frequency of specific sounds, for repetition. Games involving lists of items, e.g. *I went to the clothes store, and I bought …*.

D Classroom application

Possible ways of integrating pronunciation include:

- drilling the different expressions in *Useful language*, focusing on natural rhythm and intonation
- repeating lines of the dialogue (*Useful language 2*)
- 'shadowing' the dialogue (see above)
- identifying the sentence stress and intonation contour on lines of the dialogue
- identifying weak forms in selected lines of the dialogue
- identifying different spellings of particular phonemes, e.g. *size, try, tight*
- using intonation (rather than grammar) to make the expressions in *Practice 1* sound more polite
- counting the number of words as they listen to the sentences in *Practice 2* (to focus on weak forms, liaisons and contractions)
- listening to the sentences and repeating them
- performing the dialogues (*Practice 3*) and getting feedback, correction on pronunciation

REFLECTION

1, 2 and 3 Ask trainees to work in pairs, checking their understanding of the terms and working them into sentences that they agree on. They can then compare their sentences in larger groups. Use this activity to clarify any doubts and questions about teaching pronunciation.

38 Vocabulary

Main focus

To learn principles of word formation and word meaning.

Learning outcomes

- Trainees understand the main ways that words are related in terms of meaning.
- Trainees understand the main ways that words are formed.
- Trainees can apply this knowledge to identifying the objectives of teaching activities.

Key concepts

- sense relationships. synonyms, antonyms and hyponyms
- homophones
- collocation
- word formation: affixation and compounding
- style and connotation
- dictionary use

Stage	Focus
A Warm-up	learners experience a brainstorming activity
B Lexical meaning	analysing words in a text in terms of their meaning relationships
C Word formation	identifying the main ways that words are formed in English
D Vocabulary focus	identifying the focus of coursebook activities
E Lexical difficulty	identifying sources of difficulty in understanding and producing words
Reflection	reviewing key terminology

A Warm-up

1, 2 and 3 You can set this activity up by drawing a 'spidergram' on the board, i.e. a central hub from which several lines radiate. Write *DIY* in the centre; explain, or elicit, that this stands for *do-it-yourself* and is a British English term for home improvements; trainees brainstorm associated vocabulary, compare, and then make connections between some of the words. These activities prepare them both for the text that follows, and for the discussion of lexical sense relations.

B Lexical meaning

a   i   words of the same or similar meaning (*synonyms*)
    ii   words of the same or similar meaning (*synonyms*)
    iii opposites (*antonyms*)
    iv words that take the same (spoken) form, but have a different meaning (*homophones*)
    v   words that are derived from the same root, so they belong to the same *word family*
    vi words that commonly co-occur (*collocations*)
    vii words that are members of the same class, i.e. footwear (*co-hyponyms*)

viii   words that are topically related: they belong to the general lexical field (or *set*) of words associated with accidents.

b   The difference is one of *style*, the former being more informal and conversational.

You could ask the trainees to find other examples, in the text, of synonyms, antonyms, collocations, lexical sets, and informal style. For example:

- other synonyms: *prop up, bolster, secure; put, position; earth, ground; steps, rungs.*
- other antonyms: *up, down; far, near.*
- other collocations: *hospital treatment; domestic accidents; Yellow Pages; good condition; up and down; wear shoes; strong winds.* (Note that some unhyphenated word compounds, such as *power lines* can also be considered collocations.)
- other words that belong to the same lexical set: *ladder, rungs, steps, stiles; equipment, tools, paint-pots; shoes, sandals, slip-ons, soles, grip; hand, feet, shoulder.*
- informal style: *prop up* (cf. *support*); *get* (cf. *purchase*).

C   Word formation

1   1–b) 2–c) 3–d) 4–a)

Note that there is another process of word formation, called *conversion*, whereby words of one part of speech, such as a noun, are used as another part of speech, such as a verb. Examples in the text are *position* (noun into verb), and *slip-ons* (verb into noun).

2   You may wish to give the following as an example: *majority*: the suffix *-ity* added to the root (*major*) makes an abstract noun. Other examples: *minority, necessity, clarity, ability,* etc.

available: *-able* = capable of: *washable, reasonable*

equipment: *-ment* = noun ending: *achievement, management*

guttering: *-ing* = noun ending: *clothing, timing*

resecure: *re-* = do again, return: *replay, review*

untie: *un-* = not, opposite of: *unplug, undo*

user: *-er* = the performer of an action: *worker, drier*

D   Vocabulary focus

1   The coursebooks target the following areas:

a   collocation, specifically, words and phrases that co-occur with *say* and *tell*.

b   affixation, specifically, terms used in advertising and to describe consumer items.

c   very informal style.

2   Follow-up activities might include:

Collocation: gap-fill exercises, where students insert the correct choice of collocate; dictionary search activities, to find further examples.

Affixes: writing descriptions of products for other students to guess the product; talking about consumer preferences.

Style: rewriting a dialogue in order to change it from formal to informal, or vice versa.

E Lexical difficulty

1 As preparation for this exercise, it might be helpful to trainees to brainstorm some of the factors that make a word difficult or easy to understand. These might include: lack of frequency (hence unlikelihood of previous contact with the word); lack of context clues; not a cognate with an L1 word; a false cognate (i.e. false friend, as in French *actuel* and English *actual*).

- *bolster*: difficult – context only minimally helpful, low frequency, no cognates or derived forms
- *equipment*: easy – high frequency, derived from a common verb (*equip*), and a cognate (i.e. the same or similar word) in many languages
- *fixed*: moderately easy, although students will be more familiar with its meaning of repaired rather than fastened; context helps
- *hospital*: easy – from context, but also in many languages it is a cognate; it is also a high frequency word
- *nagging*: difficult – not clear from context, nor from knowledge of the verb to nag
- *prop up*: difficult – context doesn't help much, it is low frequency, especially in written language, and has no familiar derived forms
- *stiles*: very rare word, but it is defined in the text, so not difficult

2 Problems include:

- knowing how to use the word appropriately, especially unfamiliar words like *nagging*, *prop up*, and *bolster*
- the grammar of the word, e.g. *prop up*, is a transitive phrasal verb, and hence the particle *up* can be separated from the verb by the object (*prop something up*)
- countability, e.g. *equipment* is uncountable, but many learners say *equipments*
- the pronunciation of the word, e.g. *hospital* (often pronounced 'ospital'); *fixed* ('FIXid'), *stiles* ('estiles').

3 and 4 Words that are essential to even a superficial understanding of the text are *DIY* and *ladder*. Most other words can be worked out from context, but it may help to pre-teach *climb* and *rungs* at the same time as teaching *ladder*, and *tools* along with *DIY*.

3 Dictionary information can be used:

- to check the meaning of unknown words in a text
- to consult in order to complete a collocation 'map' or a word association 'map' (as in the first of the extracts in Section D)
- to consult when doing exercises of the gap-fill type
- to sort words into categories, e.g. parts of speech, or to rank them, e.g. according to frequency
- to check the spelling and pronunciation of words when writing or speaking
- to check the meaning, grammar, or collocations of words, when writing

For further ways of exploiting dictionaries, see *Dictionary Activities*, by Cindy Leaney, Cambridge University Press, 2007.

> **REFLECTION**
>
> Ask trainees to look at the text on Jo Thornley on page 124 of the Trainee Book, and to decide what aspect of vocabulary teaching it might be suitable for. Alternatively, they could look at a text in their coursebook. Possible areas will include: lexical sets, collocation, phrasal verbs, informal vs formal style, synonyms, etc.

39 Text grammar

Main focus
To analyse ways that sentences are connected and ways that texts achieve coherence.

Learning outcomes
- Trainees understand the main lexical and grammatical ways that texts are made cohesive.
- Trainees understand the difference between cohesion and coherence and understand how coherence is related to text organisation.
- Trainees can apply these understandings to the teaching of writing.

Key concepts
- cohesion, coherence
- text organisation
- linking (cohesive) devices: repetition, reference, substitution, ellipsis
- genre

Stage	Focus
A Warm-up	'chain' writing, in order to introduce notions of cohesion and coherence
B Connected text	recognising the features of a text that determine the way it is sequenced
C Cohesion	identifying specific lexical and grammatical cohesive devices
D Coherence	contrasting incoherent and coherent text and identifying features of text organisation
E Classroom application	evaluating and improving learner writing
Reflection	re-capping the main issues relating to the idea of text grammar

A Warm-up

The purpose of this section is both to demonstrate a fun writing activity and to introduce a view of language systems that function at a level 'beyond the sentence'.

1 Explain the activity as follows:
   'Take a blank sheet of paper. I am going to give you the title of a text. You are going to write the first sentence. When you have written the first sentence, hand the text on to the person sitting on your right. In turn, you will receive the beginning of a text written by the person on your left. Read their opening sentence and write a second sentence that follows from it. Hand your text on again. Keep adding sentences to the texts you receive, until your original sheet of paper comes back to you.'
   Set the title of the text: *The Grasshopper*. Each trainee makes up the first sentence of a text at the top of a blank sheet of paper, and, at a given signal, hands it on to the person on their right. Note that the title is deliberately ambiguous and some trainees may interpret it as being the heading of a factual text (i.e. *Grasshoppers*) while others may interpret it as a narrative (*Once upon a time there was a grasshopper…*). Avoid giving an indication as to what kind of text they should write.

One option is to have trainees write the texts straight on to overhead projector transparencies, so that individual texts can later be projected and discussed.

2 When the texts have done the full round of all the class – or, if the class is big, when the texts are at least five or six sentences long – ask individuals to evaluate the text that they started and comment on it. Use their comments to establish these points:

- Language is organised at a level 'beyond the sentence', one way being the use of linking devices, such as referring expressions (*his, their, the former,* etc.).
- Certain text types (e.g. stories or factual texts) are organised in particular ways and knowledge of these conventions helps both in their interpretation and production.
- The connectedness of texts is called 'cohesion'; their capacity to make sense is called 'coherence'.

B Connected text

1 and 2 The purpose of this task is to identify those features of a text that contribute to its cohesion and its coherence. Note that the task is easier if the sentences are photocopied and cut up, so that there is one set of sentences per group of three trainees. They can then physically manipulate the sentences. The original texts (which should also be photocopied) are these:

---

(5) GRASSHOPPER
(7) Grasshoppers are insects. (3) They live in fields and meadows and feed on green plants. (13) They can hop as much as 75 centimetres. (2) The male grasshopper chirps to attract a mate. (8) He does this by rubbing the insides of his back legs against his wings.

(11) FERN
(10) Ferns are primitive plants. (14) There have been ferns on Earth for over 300 million years. (1) Some prehistoric ferns were as tall as trees.
(6) Ferns have no flowers or seeds. (12) Instead they have tiny cells called spores under their leaves. (4) The wind scatters the spores on to the ground and they grow into tiny plants. (9) Later these plants grow into new ferns.

(adapted from *Pocket Encyclopedia* Jack)

© Cambridge University Press 2007

---

4 The following points should be made:
- Separating the texts was possible because of lexical repetition (*ferns, grasshopper(s)*) plus lexical sets or chains (*ferns* → *spores; grasshopper* → *wings*), all of which are indicators of the topic of each text; also background (or world) knowledge (e.g. that grasshoppers hop but plants don't) helps separate the two topics. (This is knowledge that is not linguistic, but extralinguistic.)

- Ordering the texts was possible because of (a) knowledge of the *text type*, e.g. that general statements, such as (7) and (10) precede more specific ones, such as (2); and (b) various linking devices, such as:
  - word repetition: *spores … spores*; *plants … plants*
  - synonyms and words from the same lexical field: *primitive … prehistoric*
  - back reference using *pronouns* (*they, he, this*)
  - back reference using different determiners, such as the definite article (*the spores*) and *this/these*
  - sequencers, such as *later*
  - substituting parts of previous sentences, as in *he does this* (for *he chirps to attract a mate*)
  - ellipsis (omitting content which can be 'carried over' from previous sentences, as in *Instead [of having no flowers or seeds]*…

To summarise, the task was possible through a combination of background/subject knowledge, text-type knowledge and knowledge of specific linking devices.

C Cohesion

1 These sentences all include references to previous matter. (See above.)

2 a The repetition of *plants* plus back reference using *these*, suggests that the two sentences are connected.

  b The learner might think that *they* refers to *ferns*, especially if they didn't know the word *hop*.

3 • repetition: (*pure*) *copper*; *metals*
  • words from the same lexical field: *copper, metals, ore, smelting, alloy, brass*
  • opposites: *soft, harder*
  • sequencers: *to begin with … later*
  • linkers: *but*
  • pronoun reference: *they, it*
  1 The first three are examples of lexical cohesion.
  2 The fourth, fifth and sixth items are examples of grammatical cohesion.

4 Extract A focuses on sequencers, such as *finally, secondly* and linkers, such as *in other words, however.* Extract B focuses on pronoun reference.

D Coherence

1 The text doesn't make sense (i.e. it is not coherent) mainly because there is no topic consistency from one sentence to the next (e.g. *METAL, copper, metals, dyes* …). It would still not make sense if we didn't know that dyes don't hop. In fact, the text is made up of sentences from other (similar) texts, which may account for the fact that it is notionally cohesive (e.g. *But … they … others … do not*), but this doesn't make it coherent.

2 1 Both texts begin with a statement, in the present tense, which identifies a defining feature of the topic (the fern's *primitiveness*, or the mollusc's *softness*) and then goes on to elaborate or develop it in a second sentence.

  2 The second paragraph introduces a new theme (*propagation* and *locomotion*, respectively). There is a general movement from the general to the more specific, or from the 'big picture' to the 'close-up'.

3 A similar structure can be seen in the *Copper* text, suggesting that these features are generic.

E Classroom application

1 1 Cohesion: the text is made cohesive by a chain of topic-related words, some of which are repeated, such as *TV, programme(s)*. There are also some linkers, like *but*.

   2 Coherence: the use of *In the other hand* in paragraph two suggests a contrast, yet it is difficult to see what ideas are being contrasted. This threatens the overall coherence and in fact it is difficult to see what the writer is arguing either for or against, although it is clear from the text type and the last paragraph that this *is* a letter of complaint or protest. The possible use of sarcasm (saying the opposite of what you intend), as in *clever and interesting programmes such as a Miss World Award*, doesn't help matters either.

2 The text could be improved if the writer was asked to be explicit about his/her opinion, by, for example, developing the first sentence. This might involve giving an example of *the programmes you are showing* and by saying exactly what his/her opinion is: *I think they are* …. Also, the second paragraph needs to be more clearly connected to the first, so the writer could be asked to say whether the connection is an *and, but* or *so* one, since these are the most common types of logical linkage. The writer could also make it explicit as to what *this horrible productions* (in the last paragraph) refers to. Reading other, similar, letters of protest and identifying their overall structure, may also help.

> ### REFLECTION
>
> Use this task to summarise the main points in the session, i.e. that there are language systems that operate at a level beyond the individual sentence and that these consist of *cohesive devices* that connect sentences and features of *text organisation* that structure texts in ways that fulfil the expectations of readers. Thus, when we can talk about *the grammar of texts*, we are talking about these larger-than-sentence-grammar systems.

40 Professional development and finding a job

Main focus
Finding work as an ELT teacher and learning how to continue developing as a professional teacher.

Learning outcomes
- Trainees have strategies for finding work and for handling a job interview.
- Trainees appreciate the importance of professional development and understand the different kinds of development opportunities on offer.
- Trainees know how to make the best use of the opportunities.

Key concepts
- work contexts: state sector, private sector; in English-speaking country or abroad
- pay and conditions
- employment: CVs; job interviews
- teacher training vs teacher development (TD)
- experiential learning; learning style, reflection
- in-service training opportunities: observation, seminars, etc.
- diplomas, MAs
- teachers' groups; online discussion groups
- TD resources, e.g. journals, magazines, conferences
- organisations, e.g. IATEFL

Stage	Focus
A Warm-up	introducing the topic of looking for work
B Applying for a job	preparing for job interviews
C Professional development	reflecting on their course experience and projecting ahead
D Learning from experience	applying a model of experiential learning
E Practical steps	planning and asking questions to the trainer relating to post-course development opportunities
Reflection	drawing up an 'action plan'

There is one optional activity which supports the unit, in which trainees consider the layout and content of a sample CV.

A Warm-up

Allow the trainees a little time to choose the three points that are most important to them. They should then mingle and speak to as many other trainees as they can, seeing if they can find anyone who chose the same points as them. Allow a little time for them to report back at the end of the activity.

B Applying for a job

1 Allow trainees a few minutes to look at the adverts and think about what qualifications and experience would be relevant. They should then compare with a partner before reporting back their ideas.
2 Trainees may think of a range of questions. Here are some suggested topics:
   * the types of learner in the school (age, backgrounds, needs, etc.)
   * the support available for new teachers
   * the syllabus and system of assessment
   * the material used e.g. coursebooks
   * the availability of computers, internet access, DVDS, videos, etc.
   * opportunities for taking on responsibility and the beginnings of a 'career path'
   * salary/holidays/benefits, etc.

C Professional development

1 The purpose of this activity is not to evaluate the course, or provide feedback on it, but simply to encourage trainees to think about how learning opportunities may be viewed and used differently by different people. It is not expected that trainees will necessarily concur, although there is likely to be a preference for the more practical aspects of the course, in terms of their learning potential.
2 The activity anticipates others that follow, so it is not necessary to go into any detail at this stage.

D Learning from experience

1 You may want to draw (or project) the *learning cycle* on the board. Again, ask trainees to reflect on their course so far: the obvious parallel with the learning cycle is the teaching practice experience, which follows a cycle of planning, teaching, reflecting, drawing out principles and planning again.
2 Elicit some ideas, such as reading, attending workshops, etc.
3 The following, slightly more detailed descriptions of the different learner types (from Honey and Mumford[1]) may help you with this task (but note that this material is copyright and cannot be copied and distributed to trainees):
   Activists like to be involved in new experiences. They are open minded and enthusiastic about new ideas but get bored with implementation. They enjoy doing things and tend to act first and consider the implications afterwards. They like working with others but tend to hog the limelight.
   Reflectors like to stand back and look at a situation from different perspectives. They like to collect data and think about it carefully before coming to any conclusions. They enjoy observing others and will listen to their views before offering their own.
   Theorists adapt and integrate observations into complex and logically sound theories. They think problems through in a step by step way. They tend to be perfectionists who like to fit things into a rational scheme. They tend to be detached and analytical rather than subjective or emotive in their thinking.
   Pragmatists are keen to try things out. They want concepts that can be applied to their job. They tend to be impatient with lengthy discussions and are practical and down to earth.

1 Learning Styles Questionnaire, www.peterhoney.com

Note, that, as in all categorisation systems, there is a tendency to over-compartmentalise and that the ideal learner type would be the one who shares *all* these characteristics.

As a way of introducing the concept of different learning styles (and only if space allows), ask trainees to imagine the floor of the room divided into four quadrants. Identify each quadrant as being one of the learning styles. Ask trainees to stand up and, as you read the above descriptions aloud, they position themselves in the quadrant that best matches their own assessment of their learning style. (If they feel they share qualities with more than one descriptor, they can 'straddle' the relevant quadrants.) They can then talk to the trainees in their immediate vicinity, with a view to finding out what they share in terms of learning style.

The activities that would suit the different styles might be:

activist: b), f), i); reflector: a), d), e), j); theorists: c), h), k); pragmatists: f), g), l).

4 Ask trainees to identify their preferred developmental strategy – and its associated learning style – while reminding them that it is often a case of having to make the best of the in-service training opportunities that are available.

E Practical steps

Anticipate the trainees' questions by preparing responses for the different categories, with special reference to the kinds of contexts that trainees anticipate working in. This information could take the form of a handout. Note, also, that the *Resource file* in the Trainee Book includes useful website addresses and a booklist. Typical questions might be:

- Are there any teachers' organisations I could join? (Answer: IATEFL, TESOL, or local branches)
- What are the benefits of joining one? (Answer: conferences, newsletters and other publications; professional advice and job-seeking)
- What newspapers and journals are suitable for new teachers? (Answer: *English Teaching Professional, Modern English Teacher*, plus many local journals)
- What's the value of joining a discussion list? (Answer: sharing ideas with like-minded teachers; immediate answers to pressing problems)
- Where can I get information about useful books? (Answer: publishers' websites; Amazon; reviews in journals)
- When should I consider doing a Diploma Course? (Answer: after having gained substantial experience, and, preferably only on the recommendation of your Director of Studies or more experienced colleagues)

REFLECTION

Ask trainees, working individually, to draw up some action points for their first few months of teaching. Obviously, their action plans will be dependent on the situation they find themselves in (which may still be unknown), but they should be able to sketch out some broad strategies for development after the course. Allow trainees to compare their plans in groups.

Optional activity

1 Work in pairs. Look at the following curriculum vitae. Discuss these points:
  1 Do you like the layout of the CV?
  2 Are these the same sections that you would include on your own CV?
  3 Are they in the same order that you would put them in?
  4 Would you include more or less detail?
  5 What information can you include on your own CV?

 John Haseley

Profile
A keen and enthusiastic teacher. Able to work on own initiative or as part of a team. Good language awareness and a dedication to helping others meet their objectives. A background in business and offers Business English as a specialism.

Qualifications
BA Business and Trade 2:2 University of East Midlands
3 A-levels: English (C), History (C), French (D)
Certificate in English Language Teaching to Adults (CELTA) (Inside Track School of English, Brighton)

Career history
Summer 2007 English Language Teacher
UK Summer School Scheme
Bournemouth
2006–7 Temporary bar work

Personal details
Date of birth: 3 October 1985
Full driving licence

Interests
Reading, going to the cinema and sport

Contact details
17 Mermaid Drive
Bournemouth
BO4 9TQ
07841 946112
johnnyhhaseley@hotmail.co.uk

Reference
Ms Ally Foster
Director of Teacher Training
Inside Track School of English
21–25 Grays Road
Brighton

2 Write your CV. Then compare with a partner. How could you improve your CVs?

© Cambridge University Press 2007

Trainer's notes for optional activity

Trainees could look at the CV produced here in small groups and compare it to their own. They could brainstorm the sections and information that they think would be relevant and also discuss the amount of detail that they think is necessary. If you have time, for example on a part-time course, this could lead into the trainees producing their own CVs.

Teaching practice

Teaching practice (TP) is a core component of the course, and provides trainees with immediate, ongoing, and hands-on experience in classroom practice. TP is an opportunity to try out practical approaches that have been described in the methodology sessions. Also, through the feedback and reflection that follows TP, it acts as a stimulus to the development of trainees' personal and practical theories of teaching. For the maximum benefit to be gained from TP, the trainer's involvement is crucial, both before and after TP, and also during it. Although all trainers will have their own preferred styles and routines, here are some points on the setting up and conducting of TP that you may like to consider. The trainer's role in TP typically involves the following functions:

- preparing and assigning 'TP points', i.e. the guidelines for each trainee's TP lesson (at least at the start of the course)
- supervising guided lesson planning
- observing the TP lessons
- conducting a feedback session after TP, usually with all the trainees involved
- evaluating the lessons and writing up, for each trainee, a post-TP report
- where appropriate, integrating reflection on the TP experience into the scheduled methodology sessions

Each of these functions will be dealt with below and in turn. But before we look at the trainer's role, it is important to emphasise the importance of establishing a good group dynamic between the members of the TP groups. Without such a dynamic the learning potential of TP may be adversely affected. Factors that promote a good dynamic in groups include:

- *having a shared purpose*: It is important that the group members understand that TP is not a competition or 'talent quest', but that, by collaborating, they have a better chance of succeeding than if they don't
- *time spent together*: Form the groups as soon as possible, and give them as much time as is possible in the timetable to work together
- *learning about each other*: Encourage trainees to share experiences, e.g. by talking about previous teaching and/or learning experiences
- *interaction*: Set up activities which require trainees to interact, e.g. group planning, group feedback
- *proximity*: Make sure that the trainees can sit and work together, and ensure that no single member is 'out of the group', e.g. sitting apart from the group, or simply not participating

TP points

Usually, the TP lessons are based on published coursebook material. The coursebook is chosen because it is representative of published materials and because it is suitable for the level of the learners. Trainees will normally have access to the standard coursebook components, including any recorded listening material, the workbook and the teacher's guide. Trainees may also be encouraged to adapt and supplement the material that they are using, but at the same time they should be able to demonstrate that they can exploit existing materials without spending an unrealistically excessive amount of preparation time.

The purpose of setting TP points (rather than asking trainees simply to follow the book) is mainly to ensure that each trainee gets to teach a variety of lesson types – including some with a language focus, and others with more of a skills focus. The TP points also serve to show – at the earlier stages of the course – how coursebook material might be segmented and adapted by an experienced teacher. And they are a way of introducing and explaining activity types that might not yet have been covered on the course. They also pinpoint the main focus of the lesson for the trainee.

The TP points should be distributed sufficiently in advance of TP to allow trainees reasonable planning time: this may be two or three days in advance in the case of intensive courses, and more in the case of part-time courses. TP points tend to be more detailed and explicit at the beginning of the course, but less so as the course progresses. By the end of the course, trainees should be able to plan their lessons unguided and unassisted, although some collaboration with colleagues will still be necessary so as to ensure cohesion between lessons, and to avoid undue overlap.

Here are two sets of TP points, taken from Day 2 and Day 6 of a 20-day (four-week) course, based on the same upper-intermediate coursebook. Note that initially the TP points are detailed and explicit, and that each is assigned to a particular trainee. By Day 6 the trainees are simply given broad suggestions. Some centres encourage trainees to segment and allocate the material themselves:

Material: Inside Out Upper Intermediate Unit 1 | 5 × 15–20 minutes

1 Aim: To practise talking about pictures

Page 4: Put the learners into pairs/threes and get them to share what they know about these events. Your role is to explain the activity and then monitor and help the learners where necessary. Ask some groups to report back in open class on their discussions. If you have time you may like to do the quiz (section 2 page 4) in open class.

2 Aim: To practise listening skills

Section 3 page 4: Tell the learners that they will listen to four people talking about the pictures. Play the tape once right the way through and learners should match the speaker to the picture/event they are talking about. Section 4 page 5: Play the tape again, stopping after each speaker. This time learners fill in the gaps in the script.

3 Aim: To revise auxiliary verb use

Section 1 page 6: Explain the activity to the learners. Do the first question in open class so it is clear what has to be done – then ask learners to work individually to write the remaining answers. Let the learners compare in pairs before reporting back in open class. Monitor and help as necessary.

4 Aim: To practise speaking skills

Section 2 page 6: The learners should work in pairs or small groups and ask each other and answer the questions that they wrote in lesson 3 – but this time they answer about themselves. Afterwards ask learners to report back what they found out about each other. If you can, leave a little time and try to correct any errors that you overheard while learners were talking in groups.

5 Aim: To practise speaking skills

Elicit from the learners what they talked about in the first lesson of the day (see above). They should then work in pairs and suggest three other events that have happened during their lifetimes which they feel are very significant. The pairs should then join another pair (to make a group of 4) and they pool their ideas and try to agree on a joint list of the three most significant events. Allow time for reporting back.

Material: Inside Out Upper Intermediate Unit 3 | 3 × 35minutes

Theme: Money

Language point: unreal conditions

Possible activities

Vocabulary: a good chance to introduce a 'lexical set' – words related to money – and to practise dictionary skills (see page 29 Lexis 1 & 2)

Grammar: presentation and practice of unreal conditions (see page 30 – Close up)

Reading: exploit the text and tasks on pages 24 & 25.

Guided lesson planning

The setting up of guided lesson planning varies greatly between centres. However, the following points may prove useful where there is sufficient time. Particularly in the early stages of the course, the trainer is usually available to advise on lesson planning, whether done collaboratively or individually. Such guidance can take various forms, including:

- observing the process of group planning, based on the TP points, and making suggestions only when the trainees seem to be in difficulty
- directing the trainees as they 'walk through' their lessons, using the other trainees as 'dummy learners': this can be useful at the earlier stages of the course
- talking through a draft of the trainee's lesson plan with the individual trainee: this is often appropriate at the later stages of the course.

Observing lessons

When observing TP, trainers need to be able to see and hear the trainees and the learners, while not being too obtrusive themselves. Trainers should have a copy of the trainee's lesson plan (although this may not apply for the very early stages of the course), and any materials that accompany it.

Most trainers make notes while observing, and will refer to these during the feedback session and when writing up a TP report. One way of organising these notes is to record the stages of the lesson, and, at each stage, to note both strong and weak points, as appropriate.

Some trainers find it useful to make a video or audio recording of the lesson, or parts of it, for later review and analysis. If videoing the lesson, it is best if the observing trainees take turns to do this. The trainee who has been recorded can then use the recording for self-assessment purposes, a summary of which could be entered into a training journal. Make sure that all trainees are videoed while teaching. (It is generally not a good idea, though, to view a video recording of a lesson as a group, as most people are initially embarrassed to see themselves on film.)

Opinion is divided as to the extent trainers should intervene during TP. The conventional wisdom is that they shouldn't, as, among other things, this might create a lack of confidence on the part of the learners. At the same time, *not* to intervene when a trainee is clearly in need of advice – such as when it is obvious that learners don't know what they should be doing in groupwork – may seem unnecessarily heartless, especially at earlier stages of the course. There are grounds for arguing that the learning of any new skill, including teaching, is a *mediated* experience. That is, it is best achieved by working in close collaboration with a more experienced other. This collaboration can take the form of 'coaching from the sidelines', as when the trainer (who is ideally seated near the trainee) prompts the trainee from time to time, or even *team-teaching*, when the trainer and trainee take turns to teach the stages of the lesson. This model of training is especially appropriate in training contexts where the trainee is sharing a class with the supervising teacher. It is important to stress that any such mediation should be progressively withdrawn over the duration of the course, and that in the last observed lessons the trainees should be both planning and teaching their lessons independently.

Conducting TP feedback

Feedback on TP is typically conducted as a group, with the trainer guiding the discussion. It may take place immediately after TP, or on a subsequent day. In either case, the feedback can be usefully structured around a *reflection task* that the trainees who taught in TP have been given, and around an *observation task* that the observing trainees have been given. (A selection of such tasks can be found in the sections on teaching practice, and on TP Observation in the Trainee's Book.) The choice of task will depend on such factors as: the stage of the course; the developmental path of individual trainees; the kind of lessons taught (e.g. whether there was a focus on language or on a particular skill); and the particular focus of the current methodology sessions. Even when TP feedback follows immediately on TP, it is important that trainees have taken the time to write a short self-evaluation of their lessons. Below is an example of the self-evaluation rubric that is used by one centre.

Self evaluation of teaching practice

After each teaching practice session you should take some time to consider your lesson and complete this form. If you wish to write more for any section, continue over the page.

Name: ....

Date lesson was taught: .... **Main aim of lesson:** ....

To what extent do you think you achieved this aim? Put a cross on the line: 0% —————————100%
What did you like about the lesson?
What would you change about the lesson if you taught it again?
Are there any questions you would like to ask your tutor?

In situations where feedback occurs on a subsequent day the use of learner journals can be useful, as long as the trainees have sufficient time to complete them. (For journal writing tasks, see the relevant section in the Teaching Practice chapter in the Trainee's Book).

It can be helpful to start the feedback session with some general comments that focus on the lesson 'as a whole' – even if it has been shared by more than one trainee, and also to focus on the learners and their response to the lesson.

When discussing individual lessons, try to focus trainees' attention away from simply what 'went wrong' in the lessons, and towards drawing some concrete conclusions as to how they can improve their practice. This may take the form of:

- **description**: ask the trainee to quickly re-cap the stages of the lesson
- **positive evaluation**: ask the trainee to say what went right
- **problem identification**: ask the trainee to identify any problematic moments
- **explanation**: ask the trainee to try and account for the problem(s)
- **possible solutions**: ask the trainee to say what they might do differently in the future

The other trainees should be involved in the feedback as well, especially at the *possible solutions* stage. But it is very important that they should not be encouraged to make negative criticisms about a trainee's lesson. One way of structuring peer feedback so as to reduce the risk of negative criticism is to provide a rubric that helps 'accentuate the positive', such as:

Complete this sentence: *What I liked about your lesson was ....*
Complete this sentence: *What I wondered about was ....*

(There are more TP observation tasks in the Trainee's Book.)

While it is important to maximise group participation in TP feedback, the trainer should not abdicate responsibility entirely. The trainer's role is to orchestrate and guide the discussion, to defuse any incipient aggression or defensiveness, to draw out action points that can be applied in future lessons, as well as to provide explicit suggestions and advice. When making suggestions, these may be more easily accepted if framed, not as *you should do X*, but as *what I find helps is ....* or *what I might have done is ....* A useful framework for conducting TP feedback is the '4S' one[1]:

S – *Sympathise.* Begin the post observation discussion by showing that you recognise the constraints under which the teacher operates.

S – *Select.* Avoid a comprehensive or global critique. Concentrate on one or two critical features of performance – areas where your advice is likely to be accepted and applied. [...]

S – *Summarise.* Be brief in your treatment of a point, offering compact evidence for a manageable element of teacher behaviour.

S – *Study.* With the teacher, give that behaviour close consideration – what happened, what did not happen, why, what alternatives exist.

One important role for the trainer is to *listen* to the trainees. Listening with attention and understanding can help mitigate the disappointment that often accompanies post-TP feedback. Some alternative ways of conducting TP feedback include:

- The trainer leaves the room, and the trainees conduct their own feedback in a group; the trainer returns and the trainees report on what they have each learned from the group discussion.
- Initially, each trainee writes on the board one thing they liked about a lesson, and one question about it – these comments and questions then form the basis of the feedback discussion.

1 from Gaies, S., and Bowers, R., Clinical supervision of language teaching. In Richards, J., and Nunan, D. (eds.) 1990. *Second Language Teacher Education.* CUP, p. 178.

- The trainer conducts the feedback individually, rather than in a group. (This is useful in the case of trainees who are not meeting the required standard.)

TP reports

There is no set format for writing TP feedback reports, although centres are expected to adopt a pro forma which they should use consistently. Most reports tend to comment on the following broad areas:

- the planning of the lesson (including the plan itself)
- the execution of the lesson, including such aspects as classroom management, pace, interaction with learners, use of materials and aids, dealing with problems and error, and the trainee's manner and rapport

As in the giving of verbal feedback, it is important that the written report is selective, i.e. it should not include so many points that the trainee is either demoralised or confused; and that it provides a useful summary of the trainee's progress, including concrete advice as to how to continue developing as a teacher. Here, for example, is a trainer's TP report for a trainee at a point early on in a course:

Teaching practice feedback form

NAME	TUTOR	LENGTH OF LESSON
Sarah Wilson	PW	40 minutes

DATE	LEVEL	TP SESSION
29.04.06	Upper-intermediate	5

LESSON TYPE

Functions – agreeing/disagreeing

PLANNING

Your plan is very good, Sarah. There is a nice balance of activities – and I really like the idea of starting with a discussion, then presenting the new language and then having another discussion. I think it'll work well.

The analysis of the forms you are teaching is also good.

My only reservation is that you may have enough here for 90 minutes!

ACTIVITY	COMMENTS
Teacher sets up survival game.	You got into the discussion very quickly – perhaps you could have 'sold' the activity a little more at the start to build interest. Still, the mountain situation worked well and the items for discussion were all credible – well done.
Learners discuss items to take with them.	This is generating a lot of language – your monitoring is generally good – but try not to spend too long with any one group – be aware of what is happening in the whole room.
Teacher elicits/teaches language for (dis)agreeing.	Good to start with the exponents that the learners volunteered and good to then feed in some extra ones – well done. You covered the forms very efficiently – great. But.... I think you also needed to spend some time on the contexts in which each would be appropriate – how formal are they? What are the differences between them? etc.
Teacher sets up discussion x2.	Very nice – instructions were excellent and good to move students around a bit. Again – keep sight of what the whole class is doing.
Teacher leads class feedback.	Very good – you handled this very confidently. You were very enthusiastic and prompted very well. Excellent to do some correction too.
OVERALL	This was a very enjoyable lesson, Sarah – well done. There were lots of opportunities for learners to communicate and you did some really useful correction. Your planning was very thorough, too. Work on: • monitoring: keep in mind the whole class and don't get too involved with one individual / group. • considering how bits of functional language are different (e.g. formality) as well as similar. Up to standard for this stage of the course. Well done.

Integrating TP

It is important that the TP experience is not viewed as being divorced from the content of the input sessions, especially the **classroom teaching** component. There are a number of ways of integrating TP into the input, including:

- asking trainees to get into groups with trainees from other TP groups, and to briefly recount the preceding day's TP, and two or three things that they learned from it
- at the beginning of a session, asking trainees to briefly recall occasions during TP that are relevant to the topic of the session. For example, if the session deals with the listening skill, ask trainees to recall TP lessons that involved the use of recorded listening material, and to reflect on both the pros and cons of using such material
- anticipating when the language area that is the focus of the current session is coming up in TP, and asking the trainees to use what they have just learned about this area to plan a presentation or a practice activity for it

Classroom observation

Classroom observation of experienced teachers should be scheduled so that it occurs at regular intervals throughout the course. It is important that this observation has a focus. For this purpose, the TP observation tasks (in the Teaching Practice section of the Trainee's Book) have been designed for use both in TP and in classroom observation as well. The observations can provide useful data for use in the 'Lessons from the classroom assignment'.

In advance of classroom observation, remind trainees of some basic courtesies. These include:

- arrive on time
- take a seat where the teacher asks you to
- keep an unobtrusive presence throughout, and do not participate unless invited to by the teacher
- if you have to leave before the end of the class, forewarn the teacher before the lesson starts
- pay attention – if you are taking notes, do this discreetly
- after the lesson, do not make any evaluative comments about the lesson
- thank the teacher for letting you observe

Trainees often express surprise that observed teachers sometimes 'break the rules', that is, that they do not always follow the same teaching procedures that are promoted on the course. You could point out that routines that are appropriate for novice teachers are often adapted and even rejected by experienced teachers, once these routines have outlived their usefulness. For this reason, trainees should be discouraged from simply criticising the observed classes; the purpose of observation is to gain new insights into learning and teaching, and these insights may be more readily acquired if trainees approach observation in a spirit of enquiry, rather than a judgemental one.

Observation tasks

The observation tasks in the Trainee Book have been designed for use both when observing experienced teachers and when observing the teaching practice classes. There are more tasks than the trainees will probably be able to use during the course, and for this reason the trainer should select those which are considered appropriate for the stage of the course, for the trainee's own developmental needs, and for the type of lesson that the trainee is going to observe (if this is known). The tasks have been sequenced to follow the approximate order of the kinds of concerns that trainees will have as they develop, starting from such basic issues as the teacher's body language, through classroom management concerns, to the more learner-oriented concerns such as treatment of error. The tasks focus primarily on what is *observable*, that is, what are called 'low-inference phenomena', such as the teacher's actual behaviours and speech, rather than on 'high-inference phenomena' such as what the teacher or the learners might be thinking or feeling at any point in the lesson. Likewise, the tasks avoid encouraging the trainees to form value judgements on the observed lessons – or at least not until they have gathered sufficient observable data. And, where possible, trainees are encouraged to corroborate any inferences they make by, for example, comparing notes with the teacher after the lesson. This 'anthropological' approach has been deliberately chosen so as to discourage trainees from the kinds of snap judgements they sometimes tend to make, such as *The learners were bored* or *The milling activity didn't work*. Whenever trainees make this kind of assessment, they should be challenged to provide concrete evidence (as opposed to unsupported opinions) from their observations.

Introductory quiz

The aim of this quiz is to introduce key elements of the course (learners, English language, teaching, and the CELTA award itself) in a fun and non-threatening manner.

Completing the quiz should take trainees no more than ten minutes. You may like to ask the trainees to complete it individually, before comparing scores in groups and also commenting on any answers that surprised them.

It is worth stressing that this is supposed to be a fairly light-hearted introduction and trainees shouldn't worry about their score. However, you could ask trainees to work in pairs to complete the quiz, if you think that this would help to reduce any possible anxiety.

After the quiz, you may like to ask the trainees to report back on answers that surprised them. You could highlight that although light-hearted, the quiz introduces several of the key aspects of the course.

Obviously the quiz should be done towards the start of the course. A good time would be immediately after the initial introductions and any 'getting to know you' type activities.

How much do you know about ELT?

As the demand for English continues to grow, so too does the demand for English language teachers. Becoming a fully-fledged ELT teacher is a long-term commitment. How far are you along the way? Are you disappearing round the first corner, or are you still lacing your running shoes? Take our quick quiz and find out.

What do you know about people who learn English?

1 How many people in the world speak English to some level of competence?
   a   about 1 in 4 of the world's population
   b   about 1 in 40 of the world's population
   c   about 1 in 400 of the world's population

2 How many people will speak English as their first language in the year 2050, according to expert predictions?
   a   between 100 and 150 million
   b   between 400 and 450 million
   c   between 900 and 950 million

3 And again, according to the experts – how many people will speak English in addition to their native language in 2050?
   a   between 100 and 150 million
   b   between 350 and 400 million
   c   between 650 and 700 million

4 Experts say that employers in Asia are already looking beyond English. Which do they consider to be the next 'must learn' language?
   a   Spanish
   b   Esperanto
   c   Mandarin
   d   Japanese

5 Who are better language learners, generally?
   a   women
   b   men

6 Who tend to pick up pronunciation features of the language better?
   a   adults
   b   children

7 Rank these reasons for learning English in order of popularity.
   a to read English literature in the original
   b for international communication with other non-native speakers
   c to travel to the UK or USA
   d to understand the words of pop songs in English

What do you know about English?

8 How many of the following sentences contain errors?
If he texted you just now, he won't again today, will he?
Dare he behave like that toward you?
She'll have finished her exam an hour ago.
   a 3
   b 2
   c 1
   d 0

9 Which of the following are not examples of native speaker usage?
   a We've been to Paris, last year.
   b Apple's 90p a kilo.
   c There's two pizzas in the fridge.
   d And I'm just like 'What are you talking about?'

10 You are planning your next lesson and you see that there is a section on relative clauses. Are you most likely to...?
   a look in a grammar book to see how relative clauses are used
   b smile to yourself because you already know about relative clauses
   c plan a different lesson – if you don't know, your students probably don't need to know either

11 You are teaching 'can' for permission – 'Can I leave now?' – and a student asks you whether they can use 'could' instead. Are you most likely to...?
   a say that you are unsure and will find out
   b answer clearly (and correctly!)
   c tell the student that this lesson is about 'can' and so they should stick to that

12 A student asks you what a modal verb is. Are you most likely to...?
   a refer them to their grammar book
   b give some examples
   c say 'no, in English we say regular verb'

13 Can you explain the differences in these pairs of sentences?
   i a. The teacher's answer was very clear.
       b. The teachers' answer was very clear.
   ii a. She stopped to talk to her friend. b. She stopped talking to her friend.

What do you know about English language teachers?

14 Which of the following DIDN'T teach EFL as a job?
   a James Joyce
   b Graham Greene
   c J.K. Rowling
   d Sting

15 In which century was the first EFL coursebook published?
   a 16th
   b 17th
   c 18th
   d 19th

16 Which teacher said of his student:
'I was greatly delighted with him, and made it my Business to teach him every Thing, that was proper to make him useful, handy, and helpful; but especially to make him speak, and under stand me when I spake, and he was the aptest Schollar that ever was, and particularly was so merry, so constantly diligent, and so pleased, when he could but understand me, or make me understand him, that it was very pleasant to me to talk to him.'
   a Prospero of Caliban?
   b Robinson Crusoe of Friday?
   c Mr Squeers of David Copperfield?
   d Berlitz of an anonymous Swiss?

What do you know about classrooms?

17 You regularly set homework and students regularly don't do it. Are you most likely to...?

   a continue to set homework in hope rather than expectation

   b ask students why they don't do it

   c think 'good – less marking'

18 Which response best sums up your view?

   a A good teacher should speak naturally

   b A good teacher should speak using RP

   c What's RP?

19 Which answer best sums up your view of learners speaking in groups during a lesson?

   a it'll make too much noise

   b it's good – as long as it's in English

   c then what's the point of me being there?

20 Which answer best sums up your view of teaching grammar?

   a I will need to translate it into the students' language or they won't understand

   b it's useful in small doses

   c I won't do it because I don't want to bore the students like my teachers bored me

21 Which answer best sums up your view of error correction?

   a I think all errors should be corrected because otherwise learners will learn bad habits

   b I'll only correct the most important things

   c I wouldn't correct anything because I don't want to discourage the learners

22 What's the most valuable asset for an EFL teacher?

   a patience

   b energy

   c a valid passport

How much do you know about the CELTA?

23 How many hours of assessed teaching will you do?

   a up to 6

   b exactly 6

   c a minimum of 6

24 Which one of these is NOT a CELTA grade?

   a Pass

   b Pass 'B'

   c Merit

25 How many words is each assignment that you write?

   a 500–750

   b 750–1000

   c 1000–1500

Answers

1 a 10 points, b 0 points, c 0 points
2 a 0 points, b 10 points, c 0 points
3 a 0 points, b 0 points, c 10 points
4 c 10 points
5 a 10 points, b 0 points
6 a 0 points, b 10 points
7 b, c, a, d, (10 points if all correct)
8 d 10 points
9 all of them were produced by a native speaker, 10 points
10 a 5 points, b 10 points, c 0 points
11 a 5 points, b 10 points, c 0 points
12 a 5 points, b 10 points, c 0 points
13 (5 points for each correct pair) i) a one teacher; b more than one, ii) a she stopped something else to talk; b the action that stopped was the talking
14 b 10 points
15 a) Familiar Dialogues, by Bellot, 1586 10 points
16 b 10 points

17 a 5 points, b 10 points, c 0 points
18 a 10 points, b 0 points, c 0 points
19 a 5 points, b 10 points, c 0 points
20 a 0 points, b 10 points, c 0 points
21 a 5 points, b 10 points, c 0 points
22 a 10 points, b 10 points, c 0 points
23 a 0 points, b 10 points, c 0 points
24 a 0 points, b 0 points, c 10 points
25 a 0 points, b 10 points, c 0 points

So what does your score mean?

0–80 You may have a lot to learn, but on the positive side – there's a long time to learn it in. Now put on those running shoes and enjoy the challenge!!
90–170 You already know a fair amount about what's coming up en route. Enjoy the rest of your journey!
180–250 Wow! You're out the blocks at some speed – well done! But remember, this isn't a sprint and there's a long way to go!

Review

CELTA Snakes and ladders

Rules

1 Each player needs a different coin or counter.
2 Players take turns to throw the dice.
3 Players landing on a question, must answer it to the satisfaction of the other players. Players who cannot answer a question lose a turn. In case of doubt or dispute, the tutor may be called to decide.
4 Players landing on the bottom of a ladder, go up the ladder. Players landing on the head of a snake, go down the snake.

Trainer's notes

Trainees work in groups. You will need a copy of the board and a dice for each group of players. Players in each group need a different counter or coin.

Suggested answers

2 Pre-intermediate

5 *Do you like* = present simple, a question about facts, habits; *would you like* = conditional construction, invitation/offer

6 Entry test, to assess the level a learner should start in

7 Am I home? Do I want to be home? Am I thinking of the present, future or past?

9 First Certificate in English

10 E.g. using a picture showing objects, e.g. furniture in a room; describing the classroom.

12 Hold up four fingers, sound out *she, is, doctor*, indicating the first, second and fourth fingers respectively and point to the third, to elicit *a*.

14 Very generally, *some* is used in affirmative contexts and *any* in negative contexts and questions.

15 Anything involving movement, e.g. action games like *Simon says…*

17 E.g. *coffee, chicken, cake, chocolate, ice cream, lemon*, etc.

20 E.g. Ask some general *wh-* questions, e.g. *who … where … when … why … ?*

21 E.g. inviting, requesting, narrating, apologising …

23 Things that the learners are carrying or wearing, e.g. keys, watches, pens, etc.

25 E.g. *If I was a millionaire, I'd buy a yacht.*

27 E.g. *ban, van; berry, very; kerb, curve.*

28 A PPP lesson begins with presentation of a pre-selected grammar item; a task-based lesson begins with a communicative activity.

30 E.g. *This is the house that Jack built.*

31 E.g. *get over, get back, get up, get on (with)*

33 Because the teacher and the learners (if connected) can interact with the content on the board, changing it and manipulating it.

35 *Mustn't* suggests that something is forbidden; *don't have to* suggests that something is not necessary.

37 / kæt /

39 One in which learners walk around, asking one another questions.

41 The first *do* is an auxiliary verb, required in the question as an operator; the second is a lexical verb, meaning (in this context) *work at.*

43 E.g. *you should, why don't you, if I were you, I'd …, you ought to …*

45 C1.

47 English for academic purposes.

48	**47** You have been asked to teach an EAP class. What does EAP stand for?	**46**	**45** On the Common European Framework scale, which is higher A1 or C1?	**44**	**43** Think of three different ways in which you could give advice in English.
37 Write *cat* in phonemic script.	**38**	**39** What is a milling activity?	**40**	**41** 'What do you do?' Explain the difference between the first and second *do*.	**42**
36	**35** A learner asks: 'What's the difference between *mustn't* and *don't have to*?' Explain.	**34**	**33** Why is an interactive whiteboard interactive?	**32**	**31** You have to teach phrasal verbs with *get*. Think of four.
25 You have to teach the 2nd conditional. Think of a model sentence.	**26**	**27** Think of two minimal pairs for /v/ and /b/	**28** What is one key difference between a PPP lesson and a task-based one?	**29**	**30** Make a sentence that includes a relative clause.
24	**23** 'Practise *have got* using realia': what could you use?	**22**	**21** Think of three items you would find in a functional syllabus.	**20** How could you check that learners have understood the gist of a dialogue?	**19**
13	**14** An elementary student asks: 'When do you use *some* and when do you use *any*?' Explain.	**15** Think of an activity appropriate for *kinesthetic learners*.	**16**	**17** Think of four food nouns that can be both countable and uncountable.	**18**
12 How would you finger-correct this mistake? 'She is doctor.'	**11**	**10** Think of a way of visually presenting *there is/there are.*	**9** You have been asked to teach an FCE class. What does FCE stand for?	**8**	**7** 'I wish I was home.' Think of 3 concept questions.
1	**2** What comes between elementary and intermediate?	**3**	**4**	**5** A student asks: 'What's the difference between *Do you like..?* and *Would you like …?*' Explain.	**6** What is a placement test?

Correspondence table

The CELTA Course units		CELTA timetable session
A1	Who are the learners?	3
A2	Learners as individuals	42
B3	Foreign language lesson	2
B4	Classroom management	4
B5	Presenting vocabulary	10
B6	Presenting grammar (1)	7
B7	Presenting grammar (2)	16
B8	Practising new language	20
B9	Error correction	33
B10	Developing listening skills	19
B11	Developing reading skills	24
B12	Presenting language through texts	29
B13	Developing speaking skills	32
B14	Developing writing skills	64
B15	Integrating skills	47
B16	Lesson planning: design and staging	11
B17	Lesson planning: defining aims	38
B18	Alternative approaches to lesson design	60
B19	Planning a scheme of work	56
B20	Motivating learners	69
B21	Teaching different levels	43
B22	English for Special Purposes	80
B23	Teaching literacy	73
B24	Monitoring and assessing learning	72
B25	Teaching exam classes	77
B26	Choosing and using teaching resources	84
C27	Introduction to language analysis	6
C28	Tense and aspect	28
C29	Meaning, form and use: the past	15
C30	Expressing future meaning	36
C31	Modality	50
C32	Conditionals and hypothetical meaning	76
C33	Language functions	51
C34	The noun phrase	68
C35	The sounds of English	25
C36	Stress, rhythm and intonation	55
C37	Teaching pronunciation	59
C38	Vocabulary	46
C39	Text grammar	optional
D40	Professional development and finding a job	85

Acknowledgements

We would like to thank Nóirín Burke, Roslyn Henderson and Frances Amrani at Cambridge University Press for all their support, guidance and encouragement.

Our thanks are also due to Jill Florent and Penny Hands for their editorial expertise and to all those who commented on drafts of the manuscript, particularly Norman Cain, Jim Chapman, Lindsay Clandfield, Fay Drewry, Isobel Drury, Leona Maslova, Steven McGuire, Gabi Megyesi, David Noble, Mary O'Leary, David Riddell, Lisa Sanderson, Sandra Stevens, Craig Thaine, Sandee Thompson, Liz Walter and Frances Watkins.

We are also indebted to the Teaching Awards team at Cambridge ESOL, particularly Monica Poulter and Clare Harrison, for helpful suggestions and comments throughout the project.

The authors and publishers acknowledge the following sources of copyright material and are grateful for the permissions granted. While every effort has been made, it has not always been possible to identify the sources of all the material used, or to trace all copyright holders. If any omissions are brought to our notice, we will be happy to include the appropriate acknowledgements on reprinting.

p. 79: Rita Rudner for the extract 'To Tip or Not to Tip' from *Naked Beneath my Clothes*, published by 1st Books Library, 2001. Used by kind permission of Rita Rudner;

pp. 109–110: Oxford University Press for the text from 'IELTS Masterclass' by Haines and May. © Oxford University Press 2006;

p. 163: Kingfisher Books for dictionary entries adapted from *Pocket Encyclopedia* by A Jack. Published by Kingfisher Books.,

pp. 167–168: This excerpt has been taken from the Honey and Mumford Learning Styles Questionnaire, © Peter Honey Publications Ltd, 10 Linden Avenue, Maidenhead, Berkshire SL6 6HB. A full online version of this questionnaire is available from www.peterhoney.com.